Effective Communication
for Academic Chairs

SUNY Series in Speech Communication
Dudley D. Cahn, Editor

*Effective Communication
for Academic Chairs*

Edited by Mark Hickson III
and
Don W. Stacks

State University of New York Press

Published by
State University of New York Press, Albany

For information, address State University of New York
Press, State University Plaza, Albany, N.Y., 12246

Production by Diane Ganeles
Marketing by Fran Keneston

Library of Congress Cataloging-in-Publication Data

Effective communication for academic chairs / edited by Mark L.
    Hickson and Don W. Stacks.
        p.   cm. — (SUNY series in speech communication)
    Includes bibliographical references and index.
    ISBN 0-7914-0861-2 (alk. paper). — ISBN 0-7914-0862-0 (pbk. :
alk. paper)
    1. Departmental chairmen (Universities)—United States.
I. Hickson, Mark. II. Stacks, Don W. III. Series.
LB2341.E43 1992
378.1'11—dc20   90-25953
                                                                     CIP

10 9 8 7 6 5 4 3 2 1

Contents

Preface

When college and university faculty complain about the quality of departmental administration, their complaints are often justified. Where do academic department chairs come from anyway? Sometimes the best teachers are promoted, perhaps taking the chair only because it is the best way to increase the new chair's salary. Sometimes the best researchers are promoted on the assumption that anyone spending so much time in research would spend equal time in departmental administration. In other cases, maybe most typically, the chair is a compromise candidate, the one who causes the least concern to the majority of the faculty and the dean.

Usually, regardless of how the decision is made, chairs are not chosen because they are good administrators, managers, leaders or communicators. This isn't so much an indictment of higher education as it reflects a simple fact: *Most academic administrators, especially at the departmental level, are educated on the job.*

For the most part, the corrective mechanism department chairs employ is trial and error. Most chairs never know they've done anything right or wrong until their faculty begins "secret" meetings to "get rid of the chair," or the dean calls for a serious evaluation and discussion of the situation. Other corrective mechanisms are sometimes attempted.

These include workshops dealing with the issues of student recruitment, faculty recruitment, affirmative action, legal aspects of administration, conducting annual faculty reviews and the like. These workshops typically concern specific issues.

Occasionally, the deans take their chairs on a "retreat." This approach often provides a place for venting complaints and frequently the dean defending his/her superiors. Other meetings may focus on the bureaucracy: submitting a budget, new accounting methods, and even faculty salary increases. Usually these meetings deal with such issues "objectively," as paper issues concerning money. Rarely, however, do these meetings provide a chair with information to explain to a faculty member that, although the institution is allowing a six percent salary increase, he or she deserves much less — or perhaps no increase. Ultimately, the most difficult task for a chair is dealing with the faculty; *the most difficult part of departmental management is communication.*

Why, then, has no one attempted to deal with this problem? Typically, most people, administrators included, believe they are good communicators. The idea that we have a communication problem is alien to us. We rationalize. We talk to people all of the time, we must be good at it; after all, no one complains to *us* about it. But maybe no one complains because no one (faculty and chair, chair and dean and dean and faculty) knows what's causing the problems in the first place. People generally do not know why because, to them, communication is a covert and seemingly unintentional process.

This book's purpose is to provide insight into the communication process as it affects department chairs. While the chair who employs the communication suggestions and strategies discussed *should* be a better budget preparer, a better faculty evaluator, and a more flexible curriculum developer, these administrative improvements are really by-products of better communication practices.

The individual chapter authors are scholars with national or international reputations in communication. Most are practicing or former administrators: chairs, deans, vice-presidents and presidents. Their knowledge and experiences are diverse. Their suggestions are based on "tried and true" methods.

The following statements reflect what the faculty and staff think about departmental chairs:

1. I can do the job better than she/he can.
2. The chair calls too many faculty meetings.
3. The chair calls too few faculty meetings.
4. The chair writes too many memos.
5. The chair writes too few memos.
6. The chair doesn't understand my area of expertise.
7. The chair interferes in my research/teaching too much.
8. The chair's forgotten what it's like to be a faculty member.
9. The chair acts too much like a faculty member.
10. The chair doesn't have enough to do.
11. The chair is a workaholic.

While it may sound like the chair can't win for losing, such is not really the case. What the chair must realize, however, is that faculty members must have some justification or rationalization for *not* getting their desired results. In many cases, the kinds of statements indicated above are typical of such justification.

In general, the chair should establish his/her position on a number of issues at the onset of his/her taking the job. Establishing parameters allows the faculty flexibility within a confined context. The following chapters discuss how wide those parameters should be (depending on a number of variables), as well as how chairs can encourage faculty flexibility and innovation within those same parameters.

Introduction

Christopher H. Spicer and Ann Q. Staton

Imagine that you are just beginning your stint as chairperson for your academic department. Being an inquisitive academic, you decide to keep a log of your first year in office to get a better understanding of how you spend your time as chairperson. The following are your notations for one day several months into your first term:

CHAIR'S LOG, DAY 99, circa 1991

(with appropriate apologies to Captain Kirk of the Starship *Enterprise*)

7:30 You arrive at the office and go to make coffee, only to find that someone left the pot plugged in all night and the machine has fried itself. [long day coming, you think]

8:05 Your favorite candidate for a job you are trying to fill calls and withdraws from the position because she got an offer $15,000 better than yours. [money isn't everything, you jerk, you think]

8:15 Your administrative assistant calls in with the flu. The two of you were going to finalize next year's budget, which was due yesterday. [where are those files anyway, you think]

8:35   A student in the only class you teach this term stops by to say another student cheated on the last exam you gave. [why am I trying to teach, you think]

9:05   The dean calls and wants a summary of all faculty publications, papers, presentations, consulting, community service, professional service, dental appointments and the names of all children. He wants this by 11:00. [ha, you think]

9:25   The media specialist calls to tell you the department's $1,000 camera has been stolen and the petty cash taken. There is no evidence of forced entry. [a fox in the hen house, you think]

9:45   Your secretary calls to say there's a group of students from a class taught by one of your part-time evening faculty who want to register a complaint that this person is too demanding. [where have our standards gone, you think]

10:15 As the rain continues for the thirteenth straight day, a teaching assistant calls to say that the roof over her office is leaking and there's a puddle on her floor. [should have stayed in bed, you think]

10:20 The chair of the university grievance committee calls to tell you that a student has filed a sexual harassment complaint against a senior professor. [surely this is not happening, you think]

10:30 You attend the weekly meeting of divisional chairs. You learn that your budget (the one you've carefully saved to buy that piece of necessary equipment) has been frozen until further notice. [next year I'll spend it all on the first day, you think]

11:15 Walking back into your building, you notice that the entire hallway in your portion of the building is covered with water from a variety of leaks in the thirty-seven-year-old roof. [needed a good cleaning anyway, you think]

11:45   You remember that you're supposed to speak to a brown bag seminar on the relationship between liberal arts education and the necessity for earning a living in a technocratic society. You can't find the notes you jotted down last night at midnight. You also can't find your brown bag lunch. [why do I get myself into these things, you think]

1:05   The dean's office calls wanting you to know that all the other departments have submitted their budgets for next year. [brown nosers, you think]

1:30   You meet with the departmental committee on academic standards to discuss the decreasing enrollments in your department's classes. Ninety long minutes later, you make excuses and leave them to their discussion of how to define "decreasing." [save me from semanticists, you think]

3:15   You walk into the Graduate Reading Room to look for a journal article only to find the library tables piled high with what looks to be a year's worth of unshelved books, journals, photocopied articles, soft drink cans, junk food wrappers and miscellaneous scratch paper. [do I look like a maid, you think]

3:25   Your least favorite colleague barges into your office to demand that you do something about another colleague's incessant whistling while she grades papers in her office. [get earplugs, you think]

4:20   The department's undergraduate advisor calls to tell you that the new, foolproof telephone registration system has over-subscribed all of your courses by 25%. [nothing like computerized progress, you think]

4:50   As you begin to wade through the paper that's accumulated on your desk during the last week, a junior faculty member sticks his head in your office and thanks you for supplying him with a graduate student research assistant. The work they did together resulted in an article ready to submit for publication and he's quite effusive in his thanks. [not a bad day after all, you think]

Recent business and management writers suggest that it takes eleven positive letters about a product or service to make up for one negative letter or complaint. The reward in chairing an academic department is somewhat different — as our fictional log indicates. One positive result, a single instance of *actually* being able to help a faculty member, makes up for a great deal of the trying, frustrating, demanding and otherwise unpleasant aspects of the job. It helps to soften what Studs Terkel, author of *Working* (1975), claims is the violence done to all who work. As Terkel writes in his introduction:

> This book, being about work, is by its very nature about violence — to the spirit as well as to the body. It is about ulcers as well as accidents, about shouting matches as well as fistfights, about nervous breakdowns as well as kicking the dog around. It is, above all (or beneath all), about daily humiliations. To survive the day is triumph enough for the walking wounded among the great many of us. (xiii)

We think a book on managing communication in the academic department will go a long way in helping to alleviate much of the daily violence done to chairs.

After a particularly trying day dealing with dilemmas similar to those listed in our fictional log, the first author is often reminded of Rosenhan's (1973) article, "On Being Sane in Insane Places." The second author, experiencing a difficult day, is most likely heard to grumble something about the myth of Sisyphus. After an appropriate amount of end-of-the-day griping, however, both are likely to invoke the Dr. Seuss classic, *If I Ran the Circus*, to explain the continuing irrational decision to remain as a departmental chair.

The two of us share what we suppose is a moderately rare relationship: we are married to one another, both chair academic departments, and have conducted research on the role of communication in the socialization of new chairs (Staton-Spicer and Spicer, 1987). Our research and experience point out that communication — *the ability to create shared understandings with others thereby validating our perceptions*

— is crucial to chairing an academic department. Taken at face value, this is a deceptively obvious and simple assertion. Of course, communication is important — it is essential in most aspects of life. Unfortunately, unlike Agatha Christie's Miss Marple, we all-too-often overlook the obvious and simple. Even those of us trained in the communication discipline often forget what we have learned about the communication process when engaged as departmental chairs.

Our subjective and objective observations about chairing definitely point to the need for a volume such as the one you are about to read. Some of what you read will be familiar. There is a value in reasserting the familiar, especially as we embark on a new job. If you are like us, much of what you read will be new and thought provoking. It will provide new perspectives on communication to be assimilated and used to your advantage. If nothing else, the essays will comfort and support you: you are not alone in the world of academic chairing.

But, what, you might be asking, does our fictional account of a day in the life have to do with the management of communication referred to in the title of this book? We think that our list touches on several key aspects involved in learning to be a chair. Although the events we listed are fictional, they are only too similar to those actually occurring in the day-to-day life of the chair. If you are now chairing a department or have chaired one in the past, you are aware of how closely our list parallels reality. Our examples fit one of the numerous responsibilities of the chair listed by Allan Tucker (1984) in his book, *Chairing the Academic Department*. These lead us to four important propositions about chairing a department:

(1) *Most of the events involve, or will involve, other people and their agendas.* More to the point, most of the incidences we note occur as the result of someone else's requests or needs. Our fictional chair spent much of the day responding to the needs and demands of others.

(2) *Many of the events to which a chair responds or will respond are negative in tone.* They involve potentially

damaging interpersonal conflicts, unreasonable demands from the bureaucracy, or have no immediate or satisfying solution.

(3) *One way or another, all of the events* (even the leaking roof) *will involve the chair's communicating with someone else.* Be it with a fellow colleague, maintenance person, secretary, student, or dean, the chair will ultimately have to communicate some bit of information, some decision, some rebuke, some praise, something to another person.

(4) Finally, our research and experience indicate that *chairs typically learn to do their job while they are engaged in doing it.* There is very little, if any, training required or offered to the new chair. He or she learns the role through on-the-job training, much of which is communication-oriented.

It is with this fourth proposition, the communication involved in learning how to chair, that we are most interested. In the remainder of this introduction we briefly discuss the process of communication and socialization into the role of chair.

Our research, personal experience, and informal talks with other chairs show that all chairs go through a similar socialization process by which we learn and assimilate the role of academic chair. As Tucker (1984) notes, very few faculty chosen as first time chairs have much, if any, experience leading or managing an academic department. We are, in effect, neophytes to the role of academic administrator. As neophytes we learn to chair through a socialization process that can be described using six dimensions proposed by Van Maanen and Schein (1979):

(1) *Individual versus collective tactics:* New chairs generally experience individual socialization; they are processed singly as opposed to being part of a larger group, such as the freshman class at a university.

(2) *Formal versus informal tactics:* New chairs experience informal socialization; they learn about their job by

doing it, not from a formal classroom or training experience. To our knowledge, chairs are not afforded a formal period of classroom or internship experience prior to assuming the chair.

(3) *Sequential versus random tactics:* Sequential tactics spell the identifiable steps necessary for learning how to master a new task. There is no such sequence for becoming a chair. One learns to chair while on the job, facing any number of bewildering random events, as our fictional list indicates.

(4) *Fixed versus variable tactics:* Fixed tactics specify that a certain amount of time will be spent in the socialization process, after which a newcomer will be certified as "socialized" (e.g., twelve weeks of Officer Training School). New chairs face a variable time period of learning; there is no time schedule that specifies when the newcomer has "learned" how to be a chair.

(5) *Serial versus disjunctive tactics:* Serial socialization occurs when a candidate for promotion is groomed for the job by people already in that position who will serve as role models. Although most new chairs assume a position formally filled by a previous chair, our research and experience indicate that the outgoing chair is seldom used as a role model. A new chair's socialization is most often a minimal form of serial socialization.

(6) *Investiture versus divestiture tactics:* Divestiture tactics seek to reduce a newcomer's individuality (e.g., requiring recruits to wear a uniform), while investiture tactics are used to empower the newcomer with a sense of his or her usefulness to the organization. New chairs are generally proclaimed to be positively useful to the university and are invested *into* their position.

In summary, new chairs experience a socialization process that is *individual, informal, random, variable, somewhat serial, and characterized by investiture.* Why are these shared socialization dimensions important in understanding the job of the chair? The answer lies in the assumptions Van Maanen and Schein (1979) make about the ways the six dimensions can be combined. They suggest that a newcomer is most likely to be innovative in his or her creation of an organizational role when the socialization process is *individual, informal, random, variable, disjunctive, and characterized by investiture.* The characteristics defining the socialization process for new chairs closely resemble those enumerated by Van Maanen and Schein as allowing for the greatest degree of role innovation. A new chair, then, is socialized in a manner that *increases* the likelihood that he or she will be able to individualize and be creative in the role of the chair.

New chairs typically enter their positions excited about the possibilities, full of ideas and fresh approaches that should lead to role innovation. We certainly were when we became chairs, as were the new chairs we interviewed for our research. Unfortunately, the university structure, vis-à-vis the bureaucracy, often frustrates the initial creativity and innovation that should occur. We found that the early months of a chair's tenure are practically devoid of communication activities characteristic of role innovation — communication activities that involve doing things differently. Chairs spend most of their communication time engaged in activities that *inform* (i.e., information gathering and dissemination), *integrate* (i.e., define new relationships within the department and university), and *regulate* (i.e., establish the chair's position and power within the hierarchy). The chair may be somewhat creative in responding to the dilemmas in our fictional list — innovative in reacting to the agendas of others — but it is not likely to be innovation in a proactive manner. The new role often mitigates *against* proactive creativity early in the chair's administrative career.

The clash between a chair who is socialized in a manner suggestive of innovation and a relatively fixed university bureaucracy creates tension. This tension, we think, is inherent in the position. It is directly experienced by new chairs as they learn to balance the demands of the position — the stresses that often accompany the competing roles of *university manager* and *departmental leader.* Without careful monitoring, the tension can lead to Terkel's (1975) sense of organizational violence.

A number of writers have addressed the real and implied definitional distinctions between managing and leading. In an article on organizational leadership, Warren Bennis (1980) suggests that managing and leading differ in a number of ways. Leaders are involved in activities of vision and judgment, while managers engage in activities of efficiency. Managers engage in the day-to-day conduct of the organization, while leaders transcend the everyday organizational routines to guide the organization.

As we said, most new chairs bring a variety of new ideas, goals, and sense of vision to their new position. These ideas are ones that may guide the department through the chair's term of office and beyond. They constitute the impact the new chair hopes to have on his or her department, the mark he or she will leave. As such, these innovations and creative ideas fall most clearly within the boundaries of leading rather than managing.

Most universities, however, seem to want managers — creative managers, perhaps, but managers nonetheless. It is the managerial role that new chairs learn first. They learn how to deal with the events logged at the beginning of this introduction. These constitute the everyday work of the chair, the efficient conduct of the department in relation to the larger university. Actual leadership, taking new directions and implementing a vision, tends to come later in the chair's tenure.

Creative role innovation, the ability to put forward creative, proactive ideas and programs, occurs after the new chair comes to understand the university bureaucracy. And, make no mistake about it, the university *is* a bureaucracy in the best and worst senses of the word. The chair soon learns the need to balance his or her role as departmental advocate (or leader) while working within a structure that is, at best, reluctant to grant innovative changes. The chair learns the value of being patiently persistent, learns how to temper strident faculty demands, learns which battles are worth fighting — in short, learns how to be a player (shudder at the thought) in the game of bureaucracy.

This is a role that many of the chair's faculty and colleagues by and large will not understand. It is one the knowledgeable and effective chair will take, however, as he or she becomes the departmental gatekeeper and negotiator. *The effective chair becomes the communication manager for the department.* Credibility with departmental colleagues, other academic administrators, the dean, university staff, and students, rests on his or her ability to negotiate shared understandings in the organization's vertical and horizontal communication networks.

The real value of the book you are about to read is that it focuses on the most important aspect of the chair's role — *his or her understanding of the communication aspects of administrative management and leadership.* The chair's departmental colleagues might never fully appreciate the potential for violence inherent in the role, never fully understand the "change" that has come over their former colleague. New chairs must learn to manage successfully before they can effectively lead within the university system. The ability to communicate wisely and well is the key to the Janus-faced roles of the academic departmental chair.

References

Bennis, W. (1980). Leadership: A beleaguered species? In S. Ferguson and S.D. Ferguson (Eds.), *Intercom: Readings in organizational communication*, (pp. 152–167). Rochelle Park, NJ: Hayden Book Co., Inc.

Rosenhan, D.L. (1973). On being sane in insane places. *Science, 179,* 250–258.

Seuss, Dr. (1956). *If I ran the circus.* New York: Random House.

Staton-Spicer, A.Q., and Spicer, C.H. (1987). Socialization of the academic chairperson: A typology of communication dimensions. *Educational Administration Quarterly, 23,* 41–64.

Terkel, S. (1975). *Working.* New York: Avon Books.

Tucker, A. (1984). *Chairing the academic department* (2nd ed.). New York: American Council on Education.

Van Maanen, J., and Schein, E.H. (1979). Toward a theory of organizational socialization. *Research in Organizational Behavior, 1,* 209–264.

CHAPTER 1

Departmental Leadership and Departmental Culture

Stanley A. Deetz

2:30 Faculty meeting to discuss ways of limiting enrollment and reducing majors.

4:00 College Chairs' meeting: report on progress of department's move to add new concentration.

To many leadership and management are the major focal points of administration. However, new chairs should focus on "leading" or "managing." For me, leading is the process of getting faculty to work on departmental goals, while still pursuing their own goals. Managing is a way of leading.

Academic departments can be conceived as small communities with their own unique cultures and the chair as a member and leader of that community. The effective chair understands his or her community and the decision-making processes that maintain the community. To better understand leadership, then, we must first examine the departmental culture.

Academic Department Cultures

To some, "culture" is something that social groups *have*, just as they have language, attitudes or space. Others see

1

culture as a "way of life," a way of thinking about group activities and properties. While both views provide organizational insight, the latter best displays the internal workings of academic departments.

Departmental culture signifies the values, norms, symbols, images and social practices underlying daily events. It provides the recipes for action and serves as a context for management. Culture describes the *invisible* background of members' thought and action. Thus, it does not directly influence ideas and choices, but represents a unity produced and reproduced as faculty interact. This allows deeper insight into a department's daily workings, showing how faculty contribute to a department's character and how leading takes place. My goal is to make this invisible background more visible and describe how the chair functions in the cultural context.

Administrative Models of Culture

Leadership and leading are themselves cultural constructions and many institutional tensions are displayed in both. The most basic tension is that between the *industrial* and *collegial* models of administration. I do not believe that this tension is an accident of academic administration but reflects a natural cultural outgrowth of "rationalization" in Western society. The history of the "chair" places it in the collegial older tradition; being a chair is not the same as a DEO (Department Executive Officer). Industrialization is revealed when we talk of "wasting" a good researcher or teacher on the chair, suggesting that the talents leading to administrative appointments are not the talents of a good administrator. Despite the datedness of the two models, we find both in academic institutions. Their cultural implications, however, run deep and determine more what the chair *is* than what the chair *does*.

Faculty desire for a good boss versus moral guidance are extreme versions of the models and point up an interesting difference. The industrial/occupational model sees the chair as a means to reach certain ends. Thus, chair evaluations tend to focus on strategic planning and efficient accomplishment of goals. The collegial/vocational model sees actions as ends in themselves, focusing on their rightness and appropriateness. We have two distinct arguments, each with its own claims and evidence. The collegial argument is heard by "industrial faculty" as naive, unaware of implications, overly critical and "merely" academic. The industrial argument is heard by "collegial faculty" as shallow, self-serving, pollyannaish and cheap.

Unfortunately, these differences stretch into evaluations. In practice, I have seen good researchers receive mediocre recommendations because they were made as collegial arguments, while individuals with weaker records received more positive evaluations out of industrial argument. This is easily traced to academic awards and marks of distinction. Professional associations with close ties to nonacademic occupations (e.g., journalism) offer many awards and those most closely affiliated with collegial tradition (e.g., history) have relatively few. Department chairs always work around these competing arguments. And, as Weick and McDaniel (1989) have shown, industrially-argued decisions work well with routine information in routine situations, but collegially-argued decisions are necessary for nonroutine information processing, allowing for original responses.

The difference between appointed and elected (or rotating and permanent) chairs are artifacts of these cultural models. A sports metaphor exemplifies how leading happens in each model, leading to a different way of thinking. In the collegial model the chair acts like a captain, selected by the team to embody their spirit and provide encouragement, focus and a voice at critical moments. In the industrial model the chair is like a quarterback, calling the plays, in charge by virtue of position, directing the team to success. I think the chair actually functions like a *catcher*, as the only player who can see all the other players at once. While the catcher may be the captain or given the right to direct, it is the position *on the field* rather than in the game that affords the possibility to lead. This concept is key to the chair's roles as accountant, storyteller and minister developed later.

Departmental cultures also differ in other respects. Departments have unique histories, they reside in different institutions in different areas of the country, and they have different personnel. They could be classified as: "big ten" versus "ivy league," large versus small, private versus public, new versus established programs, etc. While there is merit to this approach, differences rather than fundamental similarities get emphasized. In working in a variety of academic institutions, I have been struck by a *fundamental similarity* of the basic issues each faced. Focusing on the basic issues, and culture as a response to them, helps describe departmental culture and provides insight into coexisting competing cultures. Three issues are significant to leadership in academic departments: (1) the alignment of purpose and activity; (2) the organization of power and consent and; (3) the distribution of tasks and rewards.

ALIGNING PURPOSES AND ACTIVITIES

Every department faces different and at times competing goals. Goal conflict is inevitable when people work together. Academic departments differ from most institutionalized groups in both the diversity of and difficulty in operationalizing their goals (Mintzberg, 1983).

The competition of goals in the department is easy to see. Natural tensions exist among teaching, research and service goals. Within these basic categories, conflicting goals are possible: between professional and liberal arts education, basic and applied research and institutional and professional service. Further, individual goal attainment often conflicts with group fulfillment. For example, a researcher's stature is rarely enhanced through institutional service, the time spent on service is almost always a loss. Most goal tensions result from the department's being a sub-community of at least two other communities: (1) the university and discipline at research institutions or (2) the college and home community in service-centered institutions. The problems of trying to serve two masters are immense. Departments may have hierarchies based on professional service contributions, textbook production and original research, as well as hierarchies *within* different topical and methodological specializations. In some sense it's a wonder that chairs can coordinate departments at all.

Faculty members do not have to share goals to co-act (Weick, 1979). But departments that do not have no stable hierarchy. Rather than fighting over individual goals, such cultures shift or change coexisting hierarchies. This leaves the department highly politicized, filled with political games, and emergent and shifting coalitions. Department chairs move in and out of resultant coalitions regardless of their interests. *Consensus among faculty cannot be taken for granted but must be seen as an ongoing accomplishment.* This view allows flexibility and freedom and provides for quick and efficient joint action. Among faculty, however, a feeling exists that any resolution is temporary and only in effect until the next problem.

All this is problematic. Add to it the difficulty of operationalizing department and faculty activity. What is the activity? How can it be measured? With what reliability? Chairs tend to judge faculty by the most operationalizable of their products, usually their publications. However, few chairs believe this is adequate. Most faculty feel that selected and defined activities and their measurement simply reflect the dominant coalition of the moment. The hope that operationalization will depoliticize any evaluation process always fails, but its potential keeps the prospect of operationalization both appealing and elusive.

Constant negotiation of values keeps the chair from becoming a strategic planner, focusing time and energy on finding more effective and efficient ways of accomplishing departmental goals. Rather, the chair mediates endless minor battles among competing subgroups. The chair's uneasiness in decision-making is a natural result of the *ad hoc* character of most decisions. The more complex the department, the greater the number of changes in institutional goals, the greater the *ad hoc* character of all decisions. Apparent resolution on key issues around a common goal (i.e., the need for greater research productivity) frequently evaporates when applied to a particular case (i.e., faculty who call textbook writing research and faculty who do not). It's an uneasy balance between *apparent agreement* on real issues and articulating the *suppressed conflict* so that the department can reach a workable solution. It seems to me that long sessions defining and specifying common objectives and goals are probably counterproductive. They tend to raise conflicts that cannot be resolved and lead to broad agreements on goals affording no guidance. Such meetings only provide statements that can support any faculty's preferences. Worst of all, having such discussions in promotion, tenure or merit meetings give the appearance of having talked about relevant issues. The discussion is kept so general that the department never seriously solves the problems. My experience is that good faculty, even with greatly different values, judge the qualities of a *particular* case surprisingly alike. This occurs only if they look at *the* case and put aside general discussion. Less goal setting and closer detail usually makes more sense.

THE ORGANIZATION OF POWER AND CONSENT

Leadership often implies power and influence; most chairs want, at least occasionally, to influence. But *leading* is more complex. Dahl (1957) articulated power as the capacity of A to get B to do what B would not otherwise do. Usually A influences through the use of reward and punishment, possession of special insight, or access to sources of information. However, power is frequently evidenced where A need *not* influence B (Bacharach and Baratz, 1963). For example, a chair's decision may not be challenged because of fear — or, more frequently, because of no opportunity for expression. *Influence may be less important than consent.* Thus, power must accommodate (1) A's influence of B; (2) A's disqualification of B from decision-making and; (3) show how B complies and enacts A's influence and B's disqualification.

Teachers know of these relationships. While a teacher intentionally influences his or her students, influence occurs only when the learning context is not contested. The students' beliefs that the material is beneficial, that listening helps them on tests or that good grades help get a better job signify consent. Teachers know that despite power, they teach only by the consent of those being taught; students can end the relationship at anytime, but typically do not.

Chairs have the same relationship to departments. Any influence by a chair floats on a sea of often turbulent consent. Weak chairs can control the department's direction when important issues are not discussed and faculty members consent through ignorance or inaction. But lack of discussion is only one "invisible" form of power. However, before discussing invisible power, we need to look at the process of direct (visible) influence.

Direct Power and Consent. To exert direct influence a chair must be (1) "multilingual" — capable of discussing various subgroup goals, or (2) capable of building a coalition between competing subgroups and goals while still fulfilling his or her goals. A department's long term success is accomplished by the former; cliques or factions are less likely to emerge with a "multilingual" chair. However, the chair's temptation is to identify with a dominant coalition. Identification quickly suppresses most conflict. However, if one communication channel is blocked, faculty members quickly find other, less direct and often distorted and creative ways to express their positions, including reduced productivity and subversion of *selected* policies and goals. Identifying with a weaker coalition, even if they better represent the chair's goals, is no better. If the dominant group cannot subvert decisions, they bully the weaker members of the smaller group.

Influential chairs maintain independence and balance on small issues, making significant decisions outside of departmental power battles. *The influential chair defines the contexts for decisions rather than the choices within contexts.* That is, the chair's focus is on defining problems, not pushing solutions. Faculty have many preconceived positions on most choices, but fewer positions regarding the definition of the situation or problem. This power to define can be abused, to the department's detriment. Some chairs define problems as crises, thus suspending normal procedures and time for reflection. Such executive moves centralize decisions, but hamper reasoned decision-making. They also create a feeling among faculty that their input is reduced, or worse — unwanted.

The influential chair shifts the decisional context to the unique features of the situation or problem so that standard or preconceived answers do not work. In another way, *chairs asking standard questions should expect standard answers, chairs asking unique questions should expect unique answers.* For example, I was recently involved in a departmental decision about reducing our majors to a manageable level. This same discussion arose each time we received the next term's enrollment figures. After three task force reports, we weren't close to resolution and I could predict who spoke, what they would say and the issues contested. Some faculty did not seek resolution, since the crisis atmosphere furthered other motives; however, most faculty sincerely tried to reach a solution. Focusing the discussion on the question of "how we were going to cover student demand next term" quickly changed who talked and generated several innovative solutions. The long-term problem was not solved, but we moved ahead one step.

Invisible Power and Consent. The "invisible" processes of power and consent are more difficult to examine. They exert influence in part because of their hidden quality. Most chairs, and new chairs in particular, are unaware of these forces. Invisible power forms a basis for freely given consent and provides the most significant influences upon a decision. This form of power arises from four sources, each affording the chair a subtle means of exerting influence.

The first source of invisible power concerns *the definition of "real."* Reality is what is taken for granted, is certain or beyond dispute in a department. The department, college or division or institution defines what is "acceptable" by interpreting reality for faculty and staff, the institution allows them to see what it (the institution) expects them to see (Weick and McDaniel, 1989). Reality may range from perceptions about the quality of majors or faculty, the importance of professional service, to how the institution sees the department. As *shared perceptions*, they become undiscussable; they establish natural power bases for faculty members. Because of the *assumed* reality, faculty who question the department's presumption are often viewed as "out of touch with reality," as being philosophical, overly theoretical or unwilling to deal with how the department works. Faculty who do not reinforce the shared perceptions are often ostracized. In many departments there are competing images of what is real. But all departments have shared presumptions of departmental reality, many not based in the *current* situation.

A second basis of invisible power is found in the enactment of values in problem conception. Dominant metaphors often enact these values and give insight into group processes (Deetz, 1986). These metaphors establish basic perceptions and values from which evaluations can be inferred. For example, the common military metaphor enacts values of staying within channels and obeying commands. Team and family metaphors may enact the values of putting the group first and maintaining a common public front.

There are competing values found in collegial and corporate cultures discussed earlier. Evoking the terms of the model enacts values for judging actions and decisions. Thus, we have one group believing that decisions are strategic, basing their judgments of action on how well they contribute to strategy. Others may make decisions based upon the moral, ethical or principled grounds of the collegial model. When collegial groups act in strategically inappropriate but principled ways, the other group may consider them misinformed or naive, rather than informed and principled.

The enactment of values takes an even more subtle form. As distinctions are made within the department, for example, each carries a possibility of establishing *hierarchy*. To the extent that the distinctions are shared, shared hierarchies are possible. In heavily politicized departments, most distinctions set the ground for creating values. Differentiation leads to stratification. For example, when a distinction is made between writing *textbooks* versus writing *scholarly books*, or writing a text to make profit rather than writing it because it is needed, hierarchy is implied.

Third, invisible power often stems from inclusionary practices. Departments have sophisticated ways of qualifying to or disqualifying members from discussing specific topics. Some of these are obvious, such as inclusion of non-tenured faculty from certain committees. Others are more subtle. Who is considered "capable" of discussing departmental issues? I have seen instances where the entire department is considered capable of discussing the content of a qualitative research methods course, yet when it comes to quantitative research methods courses, those not considered expert in the area are quickly excluded. Additionally, certain faculty members identified with particular positions (feminist, Marxist, quantum, mechanical, etc.) find their contributions dismissed by others through *labeling*. Labeling someone often disqualifies them from speaking as an *individual* on a particular issue. Such processes empower some at others' expense.

The fourth source of invisible power comes from departmental standard operating procedures (SOP). In many departments we see what some call a *procedural fetish*. Here, substantive issues are protected from close examination by claiming that procedures were followed in reaching a decision. This is clearly seen in grievance hearings, where the quality of the decision is not discussed, as long as no one violated the "appropriate" procedures. Procedures for reaching decisions represent power alignments at the time of their creation. Not surprisingly, most procedures tend to be conservative, they maintain the power of the senior faculty. As discussed in chapter 2, procedures are powerful directives and greatly influence decisions. Obviously, we do not want to review procedures each time a decision is made; they could be manipulated by those in power at the moment. Yet, procedures always maintain certain biases and value preferences that come from certain groups. Procedures are power laden and their effects are often protected from careful review and reconsideration.

Chairs recognizing invisible sources of power can manage most situations. Manipulation of each provides a subtle source of consent in the department. Effective use of invisible power also provides a chair insight into subgroup language, in effect making him or her "multilingual." The multilingual chair can speak to each faction's goals. A residual factor of invisible power is the ability to provide faculty with subtle rewards.

DISTRIBUTION OF TASKS AND REWARDS

A chair's ability to distribute tasks and rewards is an important feature of his or her power. Compared to other administrators, however, chairs have little reward power, primarily because of the size of their discretionary budgets. Chairs have little effect on salaries after the initial hiring; merit increases and other discretionary pay scales are often small in most academic institutions and may require input from other faculty members. Even control of such tasks as who teaches what, when and with how many students, while within a chair's power, are difficult to manipulate without appearing overly punitive, thus affording only minimal power.

But, while the rewards controlled are small, they can have great impact on a department. Why do little things matter so much? For example, the spread between the highest and lowest merit increase in most departments is smaller than most faculty could earn in one day of outside consulting. Yet, faculty spend far more time preparing for merit reviews — and complaining about them later — than what it takes to acquire and complete a consulting job.

One of the difficulties of academic reward systems is the unhappiness they generate. Merit pay again provides a good example. When asked where they stand compared to others, rarely do faculty report themselves in the lower group. Yet merit systems often force chairs to rank half their faculty below the midpoint, or as below "average." In the absence of a clear comparison of products, at least half of the faculty are *defined* below their self-assessment. Not only have they lost a tangible reward, but their identity has been challenged. The same analysis is applied to released time, travel support and graduate assistant support. *The chair is not just working as part of a reward distribution system, but also as an identity producer within a cultural (department) system.* Within the faculty culture rewards rarely increase satisfaction, the distribution system actually generates varying degrees of *dissatisfaction*. Reward distributions reduce rather than boost morale. The chair's trick is not to make everyone happy — or even the right people happy — but to affect the smallest reduction of morale in the most important faculty. All reward systems make people unhappy. *Who* is going to be *how* unhappy is the issue facing the chair.

Chairs error when they believe that rewards will make unhappy faculty happy. In my own time as chair the two most unhappy faculty members got the best deals on teaching loads and other rewards. No amount of reward, however, would have been enough. The most satisfied faculty members were leaned on the most. They picked up the extra course, accepted more students or delayed a reward.

The issue is not simply fairness, accuracy of judgment or anticipation, but rather it is an interpretive process through which faculty create a departmental culture. The chair may have more control over interpretive (communicative, story-telling) processes than the reward distribution. But, if the reaction to rewards is to be understood, these processes, like invisible forms of power, are as important as the rewards themselves. Further, they can be influenced. *Symbolic processes are real.* Various social and identity values may far exceed material reward. Why else would chairs and faculty have chosen such a career?

An effective chair, then, understands the cultural milieu. He or she understands how influence is enacted in the department and how to best use visible and invisible forms of power to gain needed consent for actions and to achieve departmental and personal goals. But an effective chair must lead, too.

How Chairs Lead

Despite the structural weakness of most departmental chairs, they still exert considerable influence on program and personnel development within their cultures. I find it useful to think of the chair as fulfilling three interpretive roles:

accountant, storyteller and minister. Examining these images reveals important and yet often obscure symbolic processes by which chairs lead.

The Chair as Accountant

The accountant role is not the simple bookkeeper, paper pusher role that some chairs feel. Accountancy evokes a more fundamental role image, where the chair is an *account giver.* Chairs construct the record of what the department has done, what its needs are and what resources exist. The chair does not just record "facts" but, even if unwittingly, is actively involved in their construction — the construction of "reality."

Specifically, the chair is responsible for *constructing* the *departmental facts.* Facts are constructed in an ambiguous and often contradictory environment. Facts are produced in a relatively arbitrary fashion, with traditional guidelines applicable in several different ways. Two examples illustrate this process. Many departments have "standard" teaching loads. Faculty may be required to teach from four to eight courses a year, but within departments there is usually a fairly uniform load and standard conditions for reduction. Teaching load equality is a serious departmental issue and the number of courses taught is frequently a measure of status. A reduction in the number of courses taught is often met with scrutiny. Faculty pay less attention, however, to *what makes up the specified number of courses.* Yet, the most serious differences in load are generated by what composes the courses taught, not the number of courses taught.

Chairs soon realize that several factors make up "real" teaching loads. These include the number of students per course, number of different or new preparations per term, course level, student assistance and additional components (writing, labs, etc.) of the courses. I have seen a number of interesting formulae which make such calculations a chair's nightmare. For example, one faculty member teaches two sections of the same course in the same room at the same time, compared to another faculty member who teaches two courses, or two faculty members who teach different sections but put together, compared to another faculty team that teaches one course! Independent of how many rules a department may have for these calculations (and the construction of "fact"), the permutations are sufficient to leave only the chair knowing what counts as what and where systematic cheats have been introduced by clever or powerful faculty.

The department's ability to know or understand these arrangements is limited. The chair, in collusion with individual faculty members, constructs what "counts" as a course and can make large differences in making real loads *appear* similar. When a chair factors in questions of what counts as research (e.g., textbook writing, editing a journal or data collection) or service in teaching reduction, the discretionary nature of the chair's fact production becomes clearer. Definitions are at times arbitrary. For example, a faculty member can be spending two days a week running training sessions for business which are identical to spending an evening teaching the same material in a night course at a local community college. Yet the business activity is often counted as "consulting" and is rewarded as service, while the faculty member earns money for the service. At the same time, teaching at the community college, where a greater service is offered to the community in greater need is prohibited. *Defining, then, is central to leading because it constructs the department's cultural reality.*

The chair has similar powers with regard to the budget. While most chairs have a line item beneath-the-line budget, there is some flexibility in moving money from one line item to another. The chair also has access to the Dean for supplementing certain accounts. While faculty often complain when someone gets extra travel money, they seldom complain when new equipment is bought for the office — even though it may have more effect on the availability of travel money than the extra travel funding given to someone else. Hidden accounting practices, making money available in some accounts and not others, create real conditions of surplus and need *apparently* out of the chair's control. Additionally, when a chair has line-item control, shifting monies between accounts often gives the chair more power than the best reasoned argument.

The chair's role in these reality-defining activities is not simply that of hidden power broker. My experience is that there are always faculty who take advantage of whatever ambiguity exists in the system. They often put chairs in difficult places because they find ways to construct and reconstruct the "facts." The chair's ability to maintain definitional processes is a crucial aspect of any leadership role. In this sense, the chair functions as an external "auditor."

Before moving on, it should be pointed out that accountancy does not deny that there are things that are real. Budgets and personnel talents are real. The cultural perspective simply draws attention to the continual and often subtle potential power the chair has to define and relate things to other events, thus influencing departmental decisions.

The Chair as Storyteller

The chair is the primary messenger between diverse groups both within and outside the department. These can include upper administration, student groups, alumni, local community and the discipline. The chair is both the voice *of* and the voice *to* the department. The chair has both privileged access to outside sources and a privileged speaking role in the department. As a mediator, the chair often deals with messages that are complex, unclear and often confidential. The messenger function often requires considerable synthesis and interpretation and may be seen as the chair moving from group to group telling stories. I use story here as a narrative that organizes events after they have occurred. It shows possible relations among the events and between these events and past and future ones. The chair's story frames and interprets events, attributes motives to others and sets an agenda for seeking further information.

Chairs inevitably tell but one story. Usually it is the one most easily told, whose face value explains the most. Complex events with differing meaning to different groups tend to get simplified in storytelling. Details outside the normal understanding of a group tend to be omitted or redescribed in more familiar terms. Stories that capture the imagination of the department tend to be retold and used as frames for other events. In academic departments, like other organizations, the good story has a strong influence on decision-making, frequently far stronger than the data underlying the story.

As storytellers, chairs differ greatly in enacting their roles. A distinction can be drawn between local and cosmopolitan sayers. Some chairs speak primarily to their own department and mediate as an insider to the department. They may identify closely with one group, but often fail in a mediation role due to that identification. Other chairs become metropolitan sayers, they move from group to group with some allegiance to each. While they may be less trusted in the department, they are best at articulating the department to outside groups. Cosmopolitan chairs are like the "catcher" in the sports metaphor. They are aware of the politics of their group and of relevant other groups because they are in a position to see the field. They can speak for the department, for the dean and for the student — often at once. This role often leads to telling the dean he or she will talk tough to the department and the department that he or she will talk tough with the dean. To turn the metaphor somewhat, the chair's role is like the coach who yells at the umpire so that the player will cool down and not be ejected.

The storytelling role is important. As with the construction of facts, the academic institution has different types of information, different points of access. Some of the most powerful (though not always beneficial) moves by chairs often come in reporting what the dean would or would not accept or bring privileged information into a discussion. Frequently chairs have access to changes in institutional policy and budgets that are hard for others to access. The power is not in informational gatekeeping, but in the construction of the story interpreting the information.

The Chair as Minister

A chair often acts as a cultural minister. This role finds the chair responsible for upholding the highest standards of existing culture and managing culture change toward some future. Chairs, then, fulfill two important ministerial roles: departmental servant and departmental prophet.

The first role is enacted through service and servitude. Chairs give of their time as if it were missionary work. They put in long hours. They are there for faculty, upper administration and students. Chairs refer to this role through references to personal sacrifices, doing things for others and the thanklessness of the job. Chairs also operate as prophets. The chair-as-prophet defines a departmental vision of self-suffering and denial in reaching for "new lands." Even in the "caretaker" chair, there is a sense of the wait and preparation for the new prophet. Academic institutions are filled with potential prophets, made ready by teaching roles and salary structures that emphasize prophet rather than profit.

Both servitude and vision are critical in managing a department. But what are the realities of change? I was tempted to title this section, "On Teaching Pigs to Sing" after the old saw "Never try to teach a pig to sing. It will only frustrate you and annoy the pig." I think this pessimism arises from expecting too much regarding the wrong things, but it is partially well-founded.

On Teaching Pigs to Sing and Fish to Walk

Most departments hire faculty under different conditions, at different times, with different institutional emphases. They may have functioned admirably and aided the department's development and, owing to seniority and history, may yield considerable power. Nevertheless, many now stand in the way of continued development. Additionally, groups and coalitions advocating values and procedures that advance self-interests surface.

A common struggle for chairs is finding appropriate roles for such faculty or to initiate necessary change. Teaching fish to walk and pigs to sing approximates a chair's feeling about change and how to implement it. Fish evolved to walking in response to environmental pressures. In contrast, I cannot imagine an environment that would lead pigs to sing. The issue is whether the advocated change can evolve naturally

within the department. Much of this depends on whether
faculty are (1) open to the environment and note external
changes; and (2) whether they can let go of the current
environmental niche. Also important is the *type* of change
advocated. Faculty who have not published are not likely to
start and those who feel that research distracts from teaching
are not going to change. How can a chair initiate changes
that are both doable and nonthreatening? Proposing *differential* teaching loads, thus emphasizing faculty member identity, has more potential for change than advocating increased
publishing. The trick is to remove the implied hierarchies so
that "different" can be defined as "equal."

Ironically, rewarding faculty for what they do best produces a better environment for change than designating a
change. Change is best produced by continuing activities
(teaching, research), rather than introducing a new managerial product. Departmental changes should leave no one
a fish out of water, but develop new structural possibilities
for mutual goal accomplishment. Restructure the environment, not the faculty; environments are always easier to
change than people. Faculty should not be disenfranchised
but re-enfranchised in change. The ministerial images of the
chair in conversion and comfort are obvious here. And, in that
light, chairs should not cast their pearls before the swine.
Attempting the impossible is frustrating, energy draining and
counterproductive.

MAKING AND RIDING WAVES

Initiating change is difficult and its outcome is unpredictable. Krefting and Frost (1985) have suggested a surfer
metaphor as a useful way to think of institutional change.
They distinguish between *making waves* and *picking the right
wave to ride out*. This is particularly useful for new chairs
in departments in need of change. The inclination is to jump
in and make major changes. Most departments are sufficiently turbulent that a chair is better off preparing for
change by building relations, support and understandings to
be used when the "right wave" comes.

Most troubled departments are filled with powerful faculty who cannot read environmental signs; they do not know they are in trouble. Most chairs are not good at jarring faculty into awareness, but when a clear change is in the making they can excel at helping others adapt to it. *Waiting for the appropriate moment for directing change is critical.* Chairs, no more than surfers, can make the wave they want. Effective chairs can cleverly find and shape the issue forcing change while waiting for that wave.

Ultimately, a crisis or anomaly arises demanding a different response. Generally, dramatic decisions by chairs, such as firings or major shifts in rewards (what faculty often call the "Stalinist period"), create fear and protective measures by the faculty. Even if the chair can stimulate change, it is clear that, once begun change is difficult to stop. Old battles re-emerge and splinter groups develop desiring further change, leaving no one safe — including the chair. Faculty members who must be let go can leave with anger or understanding, depending on the chair's processing of that change. Unhappy faculty lie and distort events and the chair can rarely tell other stories, often because of confidentiality. Chairs who initiate environmentally unnecessary change take on responsibilities and create dissatisfactions very different from those guiding departments through adaptive responses to environments and offering support to faculty hurt by the change. Contriving change never works (as if one could invisibly make the wave), but patience, restraint *and* responsive action best *develop* change.

Review

Many new chairs have clear ideas of what they want their departments to be. Their self-image may range from savior, to empire builder, to righter of past inequalities. New chairs tend toward controlling everything and often over-orchestrate change. New chairs who initiate major curricular change without assessing their faculty is a prime example. Some chairs believe that curricular changes magically change their faculty, that paper changes are real. *The best chair slowly builds a faculty that can direct itself.* Personnel building, unlike paper changes, are not easily controlled and require astute cultural choices rather than grand designs.

To me chairing, whether we like it or not, is the artistic equivalent of fingerpainting. The Michelangelos of the world, with their clear and immortal dreams, should find a different medium. The role of chair often is more a muddler than a visionary. A lesson from corporate management is that opportunities frequently specify goals rather than goals defining opportunities. Departmental opportunities are unpredictable and often missed by trying too hard to force a specific plan. Chairs with fixed goals frequently fall into the logic that if one is good, more is better. Guidance by opportunity, not design, seems most appropriate for a changing department.

Emerging and changing visions require that the chair's identity be invested in letting the department emerge as what it is best. The chair must often be humble. Visionary chairs often get trapped in their own self-importance. It is *their* vision and everyone works for them. Normal duties are beneath them, they are always too busy planning, and all problems and conflicts are inconveniences. Not only is this an ineffective means of generating commitment and effort, but it cuts the chair off from the department. Enacting a servant role at critical times can avoid many long-term problems. Failing such a role leads to a lack of allegiance and problems, often transforming chairs from leaders to insecure bullies. As a chair, simple acts of asking students how they are doing and reading a faculty member's recent article or paper often affect the feelings, effort and good will of all.

Summary

This chapter examined the process of departmental leadership by conceptualizing departments as cultures. These cultures differ greatly due to different administrative models, largely collegial or corporate, and the way their alternative purposes are aligned, power and consent are organized and rewards and tasks are distributed. From this perspective, leadership and leading is seen as a complex process of influence through various sources of power which arise in different ways in different institutional cultures. The most significant of these arise out of largely invisible sources. Such sources are usually more important than the chair's specific characteristics or arguments. Three interrelated images of leading are presented to help understand the process of influence and change. Hopefully, understanding such processes can help chairs achieve their own goals, while helping the department with its own open self-determination.

References

Bacharach, P., and Baratz, M. (1963). Decisions and nondecisions. *American Political Science Review, 57,* 632–642.

Dahl, R. (1957). The concept of power. *Behavioral Science, 2,* 201–215.

Deetz, S. (1986). Metaphors and the discursive production and reproduction of organization. In L. Thayer (Ed.), *Organization-communication: Emerging perspectives, I* (pp. 168–182). Norwood, NJ: Ablex.

Krefting, L., and Frost, P. (1985). Untangling webs, surfing waves, and wildcatting: A multi-metaphor perspective on managing organizational culture. In P. Frost, L.F. Moore, M.R. Louis, C.C. Luncberg, and J. Martin, (Eds), *Organizational culture* (pp. 155–168). Beverly Hills, CA: Sage.

Mintzberg, H. (1983). *Power in and around the organization.* Englewood Cliffs, NJ: Prentice Hall.

Weick, K. (1979). *The social psychology of organizing,* 2nd edition. Reading, MA: Addison-Wesley.

Weick, K., and McDaniel, R. (1989). How professional organizations work: Implications for school organization and management. In T. Sergiovanni and J. Moore (Eds.), *Schooling for tomorrow: Directing reforms to issues that count* (pp. 330–354). Boston: Allyn and Bacon.

CHAPTER 2

Establishing Effective Relationships with Faculty and Staff

Anita Taylor

8:00　Weekly staff meeting. Discussion about graduate
students' requirements of staff personnel.

9:45　Met with specialization heads to discuss new policies
on adjunct instructors.

The American academic institution belongs in a class of
organizations often described as organized anarchies (Cohen
and March, 1974). This is an apt description for many who
work within such organizations, though they often doubt the
organized descriptor. Thus, discussing how department chairs,
in performing middle management roles within such institutions, manage communication within the anarchy poses a
formable challenge. In the proverbial English manner, most
chairs muddle through the task.

Certainly, a major part of the chair's role is establishing
effective relationships with faculty. A major part of that task
involves effective communication. Though neither communication nor relational skills are ordinarily job requirements
when chairs are selected, attention to the management of
interpersonal communication within departments may be
long overdue. Although attention has focused on the various

tasks that administrators must accomplish, none has been devoted specifically to communication and relationships within departments. This chaper focuses on the chair's managing of relationships within the department.

Factors Affecting Development of Relationships

The chair's development of faculty and staff departmental relationships is affected by many factors. The chair's position is largely one of leadership. Part of this role involves paper pushing. In my more than fifteen years as chair, I described this to others as "administrivia," which unfortunately is essential. Without this movement of paper (the oil of institutional machinery), the mechanism of the institution would grind to a halt. For example, class schedules must be printed and payrolls prepared. Yet, these duties are not at the heart of the chair's role. As academic institutions are primarily devoted to learning, the chair's most important duty is doing what enhances learning. Thus, the essence of the chair's role is whatever behaviors (1) influence faculty to do good teaching, scholarship, and service; or (2) encourage students to learn. *These are leadership behaviors.*

Leadership requires that relationships be defined and maintained between the chair and his or her faculty and staff. *Appropriate* relationships vary greatly from situation to situation and from person to person. In the same way, different kinds (or styles) of leadership work in different situations and for different kinds of people. Most leadership theory distinguishes between leaders who emphasize or excel at tasks versus relationships. Typically, most of us are better at one of the two. Of importance to this chapter is an understanding that *chairs also differ in the kinds and importance of relationships they establish with faculty and staff.* Effective chairs have learned this.

Many situations, such as making merit raise decisions, strain departmental relationships. A chair who wants to establish collegial relations with faculty and staff soon finds these situations difficult. In contrast, there are situations in which success, especially in providing leadership to senior faculty — essentially autonomous professionals — depends heavily on establishing collegial relationships. Chairs who ignore the relationship-building aspects of their roles have significant problems in such a situation.

What is stressed here is *variability*. Some effective chairs are loved by all and that is important to them. Other, equally effective chairs are not loved at all; the absence of affection does not disturb them. Commonalities do exist, however. Well-liked chairs must be minimally competent, while unloved but effective chairs are almost always respected and almost never despised or greatly distrusted. However, any *significant* amount of mistrust between faculty, staff and chair interferes with the effectiveness of all. Thus, *effective chairs seek relatively trusting relationships of mutual respect that enhance the learning, teaching, scholarship and service that occur within their departments.*

What both chairs and others within a department want most is for the chair to do the many tasks focused on in other chapters in this book. Few faculty are particularly concerned about developing close relationships with their chair. What they want is a chair who arranges fair teaching schedules and loads, adequate office space and salary and who contributes to gaining respect and reward for the department. At the same time, chairs can benefit from being reminded of the factors to consider when establishing relationships that are appropriate — appropriate for the chair and the situation. Some, but not all, of those factors are explored in this chapter.

Factors Differing By Situation

A major factor affecting faculty and staff relationships is the chair's role itself. Chairs' tasks inherently involve behaviors tending to cause defensive behavior, which affect their ability to communicate openly with faculty and staff. Chairs who possess any power or authority must evaluate their staff, make suggestions about how others behave and control or limit faculty and staff activity. When put in a defensive situation, no matter how effective a communicator a chair is, faculty and staff are pressured to filter what and how they say. Because they evaluate and control, effective chairs balance both by avoiding the most destructive behaviors that lead to defensive reactions: attitudes of superiority, dogmatism and narcissism.

Other important factors influencing the development of relationships with faculty and staff are characteristics of the chair's personal style. Because personal styles vary almost infinitely, cataloging the different personality types is beyond the scope of this chapter and has limited utility. More information on leadership styles and characteristics is available in popular and scholarly sources, both in communication and management (e.g., Bennett, 1983; Fiedler et al.,1977; Gordon, 1977; Likert, 1967; Peters & Waterman, 1982).

To develop appropriate relationships, chairs should express their ideas in ways that can be understood by others, yet limit defensiveness. To do so also involves listening to others. Again, this chapter is not meant to catalog good personal communication skills. The chair desiring that sort of guidance can turn to several good sources (e.g., Jandt, 1975, 1989; O'Connell, 1979; Taylor, 1989). This chapter concentrates on what I see as the most important factor of all, the situation. Situation involves not only departmental characteristics and interaction patterns, but also the organizational culture and rules within which the department exists, the personalities and habits of senior administrators and of the faculty and staff, plus all other aspects of the setting. These include such obvious factors as: size of department, size of institution, amount of staff support, distribution of grant monies with related support, faculty support from outside sources, faculty relationships with outside people.

I will attend primarily to the factors of situation largely because, as noted in chapter 3, the idea of "the" chair's role is illusory. While most chairs do similar things — develop and maintain class schedules, monitor budgets, make personnel recommendations, communicate departmental needs to administration and information from administration to faculty and staff, deal with students complaints, etc. — no common list of such duties exists among all institutions. More important, no commonality in construing or carrying out such duties exists. Yet, their outcome determines what are considered "appropriate" faculty and staff relationships and how they develop. Thus, perhaps most important for chairs to know: *What is the culture of his or her institution and department? What are the written and unwritten rules of the individual situation?*

VARIATIONS OF AUTHORITY AND POWER

Major situational differences involve the amount of authority and/or power the chair wields. And, by this I mean *position power*, not individual or personal power. Variations in personal power exist and affect how chairs communicate, but such power is largely a result of developing relationships, not a factor to consider here. In some institutions, chairs have little or no authority, no position power. The chair's role in such institutions may be proscribed from either direction: faculty or administration. Some institutions are administered so that the chair's duties are largely clerical; they carry out institutional policies or administrative directives. Others are organized so that a relatively small group of senior faculty hold most of the authority and/or power to make important decisions about departmental affairs. In this case, the chair's duties again are largely clerical, unless he or she is a major player in that group of senior faculty.

Departments where the faculty themselves maintain power are characterized as self-governing. Typically, tenured faculty develop curricula and approve any alterations in them, hire new faculty, evaluate existing faculty, make retention and promotion decisions and often set their own schedules. Zero- or need-based budgets do not exist. Rather, budgeting is merely a continuation or extrapolation from allocations of the previous year, so a chair's influence does not even include the power of the purse. And, while chairs are expected to handle student complaints about classes or professors, they have little authority to do more than listen. In some situations the chair cannot even hire or fire departmental staff, clerical or otherwise.

In these situations, *chairs lead through persuasion and their most effective relationships are collegial.* Their effectiveness stems from faculty and staff willingness to listen or motivation to emulate the leader. Fiedler, et al. (1977) suggest that in these situations, especially if combined with an unfavorable situation (one confronting many chairs as they wrestle with student and resource problems), a task-oriented chair performs best. In a situation only moderately unfavorable, and in which task ambiguity is high, Fiedler argues that the relationship-oriented chair performs best.

At the other end of the authority/power continuum are situations where chairs have high position power. They can hire and fire, make unilateral decisions about promotion, merit pay and budget recommendations, set class schedules and assign faculty to them, etc. As such, how the chair behaves directly impinges on faculty and staff life; how they respond to such control strongly impacts relationships. Some people are comfortable with and accept with trust the authority relationships such a hierarchical arrangement involves. Most faculty dislike having so little control over their lives and react negatively to both the situation and the chair. Chairs who need to establish relationships with faculty and staff are often uncomfortable with the inevitable mistrust engendered by this hierarchical, top-down control. If the situation cannot be changed, relationship-oriented chairs probably should get out of chairing. Only task-oriented people, for whom relationships are less important, find such situations tolerable.

OTHER SITUATIONAL VARIATIONS

Another situational element constitutes a set of relationships with which chairs must be concerned: Chairs must work within the constraints established by other, senior administrators. The style of dean, vice president or provost and/or president influences a chair's management of interpersonal relations. The chair with a senior administrator who demands unquestioning loyalty in subordinates operates within a different framework than the chair whose administrative superiors are collegial. Some senior administrators can be argued with; others do not tolerate such behavior. Some deans see themselves as head of a leadership *team* where chairs are contributing co-equals; others expect the chair to gain faculty and staff compliance to administration policies, goals and plans.

Situations also differ in institutional and department maturity. Young or changing institutions involve different elements of relationship-building from long established or stable institutions. Situations may differ by many factors. Are faculty tenured? Have they established interaction and internal leadership patterns? Is there regular infusion of new faculty who may challenge previously established ways of doing things? Does the chair rotate among a stable group of senior faculty? Are one or more faculty senior to the chair? Are some staff members (a departmental secretary, for instance) senior to most faculty? Are institutional changes affecting faculty differently? These and other questions relating to the stability and maturity of the institution or department affect a chair's communication management.

Factors Relevant to All Situations

Some effective relationship factors vary little from situation to situation. These are personal characteristics that develop the credibility required to effectively carry out a role that affects the lives of others. These characteristics are especially important for chairs whose position power is high: chairs who can hire and fire, who determine salary and dictate class schedules.

PREDICTABILITY, COMPETENCE, AND INTEGRITY

First, and above all else, *the chair must be predictable.* Since a chair's behaviors impinge on the freedom of others, predictable chairs are often tolerated and respected even by faculty and staff who disagree with what the chair does.

Next, and related to being predictable, a chair must display *competence at paper pushing tasks:* scheduling, evaluating, budgeting, implementing payroll, etc. Although the skill level associated with "minimal" competence varies from person to person and situation to situation, once having learned those levels, the chair must meet them. No matter how much the chair is liked, it will be difficult, if not impossible, to maintain appropriate relationships with faculty and staff who perceive the chair as incompetent.

Closely related to predictability is a chair's *integrity*, which is more than personal honesty. A chair must do and know many things that involve confidentiality, such as salaries, work assignments, leaves and others' personal goals and/or problems. Faculty and staff must believe their chair can be trusted to maintain such confidences. Although faculty need not disclose details of their personal lives to each other, often the chair is required to obtain certain personal information. The department must believe that this information remains confidential.

An element of integrity is the perception that the chair treats all department members *fairly*. Few department members expect everyone to receive equal treatment — most believe that rank does have its privileges — but most expect that the differences are distributed fairly. Clearly, what is defined as "fair" will vary, and each chair needs to learn how his or her faculty and staff see it. In some areas faculty and staff do expect *equal* treatment. All expect to get accurate and consistent information. Chairs who share institutional or private gossip with some faculty and not with others are often perceived as dishonest and treating department members unfairly. All expect consistent application of institutional and departmental "rules." Faculty also expect some say about their work schedules and the content of their courses.

STUDENT COMPLAINTS AND INTEGRITY

Student complaints is a situation requiring integrity. Often student complaints deal with faculty. Chairs must listen to students' complaints and should listen as openly and empathically as possible. Often no more is required. As a chair, I found this part of the job the most demanding. Student complaints often result from frustration for not doing as well as they would like. But, in a competitive and increasingly litigious culture, students find it easier to blame circumstances or faculty for their own shortcomings. Rather than admit that they did not study hard enough, or were taking too many courses while working too many hours, students blame the instructor and appeal their grades. With skill, a chair may help students to accept their responsibility for the situation. Many faculty were selected as chairs, however, because of strong academic records and organizational skills, not empathy skills. As such, chairs often respond analytically and prescriptively, rather than with understanding.

More serious, however, is how to be fair to both the student and faculty member in such a situation. If a chair succeeds, through empathic listening or analytical persuasion, in convincing the student that he or she is wrong and the faculty member is right, there is little problem. Usually, however, students are not convinced, often because both have contributed to the problem. In such cases, the chair wants to be fair to the student and yet to ensure that the problem does not repeat itself. Doing this is not a simple task. Students are often afraid of faculty reprisal and fear talking to the chair. To counter this, chairs need to assure students of their confidentiality in such matters, which is no easy task. Most students unhappy or confident enough to complain to the chair are easily identified by faculty members. At the same time, in fairness to faculty, student complaints cannot be accepted at face value; faculty deserve an opportunity to refute or at least tell their side of the story. In cases where the faculty member's actions are problematic and require "corrective" action, his or her defensiveness also interferes when talking about the problem.

There is no consensus about how to cope with this dilemma. Several approaches are reasonable, all involving the basic characteristics detailed earlier: competence, integrity and predictability. Faculty *deserve* to know when a student complains about their teaching. Most faculty want to teach well, and student complaints indicate some difficulty in their achieving that goal. Faculty can improve their teaching better with feedback telling them what they have done right *and* wrong. So, *faculty should be told about student complaints, but with the student's name withheld.* Sometimes, however, the ethics of confidentiality and the chair's responsibility to the student require a delay in telling about a complaint, until grades are reported, for example. But, while some delays are justified, a chair must never "sit" on a student complaint.

A more sensitive class of student complaint involves behavior that qualifies as harassment, sexual or otherwise. Rarely is harassment overt, and even more rarely is it done deliberately. It is, however, a major factor affecting departmental relations and directly involves the chair. Problems of harassment are not limited to faculty-student interaction; staff or junior faculty can be harassed by colleagues or senior faculty. What is recommended for handling student complaints is reflected in staff or faculty complaints. *Regardless of who complains, any cases of harassment, or behaviors that demonstrate faculty or staff insensitivity to such matters, require the chair's immediate attention.*

The power differential between faculty and students (or between faculty or staff) is immense. Faculty must learn how their words and actions are perceived, even when not intended as harassment. They should realize that harassment occurs in and out of the classroom. For instance, a student may express disagreement or concern, only to be responded to with a joke. Rather than seeing the joke as funny, the potential victim may see it as reinforcing the power differential through sexual innuendo. Other common examples with the potential of harassment include faculty keeping unusual office hours or limited availability to some students, keeping some students waiting while exchanging small talk with others, inappropriate attentions and physical closeness and attempts at crude humor.

At the same time, some students charge harassment to intimidate or "get even" with faculty. It requires special sensitivity on the chair's part to distinguish between sincere and spurious complaints. Since such efforts are rarer than actual harassment — and because the definition of harassment relies on those who perceive it — no charge or complaint suggesting harassment can be ignored.

No one answer exists about what to do in such situations. Help is found in chapter 4 of this book, in student personnel publications and through the institution's personnel department. Before doing or saying anything (other than assuring students that their concerns are serious and will be investigated), a conversation with the dean, academic affairs officer or equal employment officer (in cases involving faculty or staff complaints) is a good idea. But, whatever the situation, inactivity is inappropriate. A response is necessary. The point is not what to do in such situations — the chair must act — but that competence, integrity and predictability are essential chair characteristics for successfully dealing with such delicate and serious problems.

SHARING INFORMATION

Beyond the factors of authority and control and personal characteristics is the matter of information flow. The chair occupies a gatekeeper role with regard to information. And, since academic institutions are largely information businesses with faculty professionals in that business, the appropriate flow of information is important. For most chairs, this factor is obvious. It is important to remember, however, that faculty and staff often view efforts the chair sees as extensive as inadequate. Continual effort to inform the department of what the chair knows is essential.

An important information function is to ensure that faculty know institutional priorities, policies and procedures. Because this information is often available elsewhere — and is someone else's "responsibility" to distribute it — chairs often assume that faculty and staff will learn it from those sources. And, while most chairs recognize their informational role in new faculty orientation, they too often forget that information flow must be constantly attended to.

A major source of distrust among faculty and staff stems from lack of information. Information about motives, goals, and facts is relevant to how they live their work lives. If faculty and staff do not perceive that they are receiving adequate information about such subjects, they usually fill in the gaps, making hasty assumptions of motives and often drawing negative conclusions. Chairs should converse regularly (both listening and talking) with faculty and staff. The dialogue should cover goals, commendations for things done well and an examination of what could be done better by both chair and faculty or staff member. Chairs need to state specifically what their expectations are for individual performance.

Too often faculty-chair conversations are limited to small talk, to issues of institutional gossip or to specific matters that need doing, such as setting the next term's schedule. They should share positive and negative information. Chairs often avoid unpleasant information. But, more sadly, chairs rarely comment when a faculty or staff member has done something well. In academic environments, we have come to expect excellence. Often, chairs forget how much one's sense of personal worth, even for professionals, depends on receiving positive reinforcement from peers and superiors. Thus, it is an important function for the chair to give continuing attention, both privately and in public, to superior work.

Perhaps more problematic is how to ensure that faculty and staff have the information they need to do their work. All chairs are aware that faculty need information about administration goals, policies, procedures, directions, etc. But how? There are departments where faculty and staff know very little beyond rumor. There are institutions overrun with paper, where memoranda, newsletters, information alerts and reports proliferate into piles of unread paper, while faculty remain uninformed. And, there are departments where faculty and staff attend interminable meetings which involve little except a chair saying what could have been more efficiently transmitted in writing.

Finding an appropriate balance of information is difficult. *For important information, it is best to write and say what needs emphasizing and what must be remembered.* For lesser items, writing is the most efficient way to respect faculty time and intelligence. This is even more true when the information requires a response (e.g., "Commencement seats must be reserved by Friday the 19th. Who plans to attend? Tear the bottom of this page to respond and I will notify the registrar how many seats to hold for the department.") Memos and notes that are informative and humorous are more likely to be read and do a better job of informing. Often, information, whether written or spoken, needs discussion to clarify the issue or a group decision is needed to ensure an appropriate response. In these cases, a faculty and/or staff meeting is necessary.

A second important information role for the chair is *talking regularly with faculty and staff about how their personal goals relate to those of the institution and department.* Even tenured faculty, who are largely autonomous professionals, find growth and development unsatisfactory in departments or institutions that do not fit with their personal goals. Because of their position within the institution's formal communication networks, chairs are in the best position to help faculty and staff understand those fits and decide whether this is the appropriate institution to call "home."

DEALING WITH ADJUNCT FACULTY

As institutions use more part-time employees, dealing with adjunct faculty consumes more of the chair's time. Too often adjunct faculty have little contact with the department beyond their classroom. Such faculty know little about the institutional culture and seldom understand how their class fits into the overall program or major.

While adjunct faculty have different information needs than full-time faculty, effective chairs make sure that they understand the institution and department well enough to do the jobs any faculty member does beyond the classroom. Adjunct faculty, at the minimum, should be able to answer some questions regarding the department or courses and refer students with problems or questions to the appropriate offices. They need to understand how their course fits into the overall curriculum and what policies govern their relationships with students, faculty, staff and administrators. Chairs should not assume that the adjunct faculty member has been educated on the norms of academe or has previously taught in an academic institution. Because it is hard to arrange meetings, chairs seldom have time to meet with part-time faculty members regularly. Thus, the important task of informing part-time faculty about what they are to do and how it fits into departmental goals and program often is not accomplished.

Because it is difficult to communicate with adjunct faculty, *chairs might consider delegating the task to a senior faculty member.* Release time is a small price for the increased quality of adjunct faculty-student interaction resulting when part-timers are well-informed and well-integrated into the department. The question of faculty development for part-time faculty has been addressed at length in a number of sources and is worth attention from any chair with significant numbers of adjunct faculty (e.g., Leslie, Kellams and Gunne, 1982; Taylor, 1986).

Relations Among Faculty and Staff

An important factor in departmental relationships is the role a chair plays in fostering appropriate relationships among departmental members. In many institutions, department members do not consider each other as close personal friends nor do they socialize outside the office. In other institutions, such relationships are expected. If the latter characterizes the chair's situation, it is important to understand that the organizational culture requires the chair to develop such *friendships.*

But, regardless of the situation, integrity on the part of the chair should be mirrored in the dealings of faculty with one another. Even if we have not worked in departments where cabals and internecine warfare characterize daily life, we have all heard stories of such situations. And, while no chair can be held responsible for eliminating or preventing such behavior (faculty, after all, have their own personalities not subject to control by a chair even in the most authoritarian settings), the chair's influence in reducing the likelihood and persistence of conflict between faculty or staff members is considerable. Thus, the following three principles are offered, not as cures or preventatives, but as ideas chairs can use to avoid warfare among faculty and staff.

First, *chairs should ensure that all faculty have equal access to important information and treat all faculty fairly.* Second, *involve faculty in real problem-solving,* not on every small issue of departmental procedure (of which they should be informed) but on the important issues that affect their academic lives. If, for example, the department faces an FTE (full-time equivalent) "crisis" (too few faculty and too many students, or vice versa), unilateral actions on the chair's part are not the most effective means of dealing with the crisis. Since such a situation inevitably affects how faculty do their jobs, they should be as involved in developing solutions as possible. Third, *chairs need to understand their institutional culture and their faculty and staff well enough to know when meetings are needed.* Faculty time in meetings or committees should never be wasted with matters that can be handled more efficiently in other ways. In cases where the matters are important, where outcomes affect how faculty teach, work or related to each other, faculty should help set departmental policies and procedures and decide how to implement these policies. *Finding the line between situations that demand faculty involvement and those that do not is not easy, but it is one of the most important things an effective chair does.*

Differences for Staff

Throughout this chapter issues of relationships have focused on either faculty or staff. In most relational matters between chair and department members, dealing with faculty and staff differ little. Regardless of their titles, people should be treated with integrity, consistency and be involved in deciding matters affecting their work. Yet, there are differences between faculty and staff. In most institutions, non-faculty are not expected to be involved in formal decision-making. Indeed, in many institutions, only tenured faculty make such decisions. And, while that kind of limitation may be appropriate for curricular and institution-wide matters, the same limitations do not — and should not — apply to other matters concerning departmental life. Effective staff work is essential to accomplish departmental goals. Staff members are often highly skillful in public contact and do more than most faculty to establish the tone and attitude by which the department is known to outsiders.

Staff members (like faculty) must be competent at their jobs. If they are not, the chair must know how to deal with them. Chairs must know what corrective actions are available. (Does the institution have a policy or contract that guides how staff should be treated?) Similarly, chairs must be able to consult with and evaluate or reprimand staff members just as they do faculty. Chairs who cannot do this create problems for themselves and their departments.

Staff should not be treated as servants, even though their roles may be largely service. Clear job descriptions, written (or modified) to specifically apply to the particular situation, are necessary. So, too, is regular, open and honest communication. The question of staff roles and their relations with faculty is a matter that often requires the chair's attention. Too many faculty are intellectual snobs who consider themselves more important (therefore more valuable) than the staff. Coping with this perception is not easy for chairs, who are themselves faculty. *Effective faculty and staff relations are essential because, without high quality staff service, most departments (not to mention their chairs) are in great difficulty.* Though academic institutions by nature are elitist institutions, the chair needs to remember that staff play essential roles in accomplishing departmental goals. They earn faculty respect and decent treatment; it is the chair's task to see that they get it.

Summary

In the final analysis, establishing and maintaining effective relationships within one's department requires the wisdom of Athena, the intelligence of an Einstein and the saintliness of a Ghandi. Since few chairs possess even one of those traits, they do as indicated, the best they can to be competent at the paper tasks of the job and decent human beings. This, in turn, makes them competent at the people tasks of chairing. Not much more can be asked, nor is it needed.

This chapter has focused on establishing working relationships with faculty, staff and students. Effective chairs understand their institution's culture and the type of relationships expected of them. Although there are a variety of factors involved, effective chairs possess a sense of personal integrity and are perceived as competent and predictable by their peers and subordinates.

References

Bennett, J.B. (1983). *Managing the academic department: Cases and notes.* New York: American Council on Education. Macmillan.

Cohen, M.D., and March, J.G. (Eds.) (1974). *Leadership and ambiguity: The American college president.* Cambridge, MA: Harvard Business School Press.

Fiedler, F., Chemers, M., and Marar, L. (1977). *Improving leadership effectiveness: The leader match concept.* New York: Wiley.

Gordon, T. (1977). *Leader effectiveness training.* New York: Bantam Books.

Jandt, F. (1973). *Conflict resolution through communication.* New York: Harper & Row.

Jandt, F. (1985). *Win/win negotiating.* New York: Wiley.

Leslie, D., Kellams, S., and Gunne, M. (1982). *Part-time faculty in American higher education.* New York: Praeger.

Likert, R. (1967). *The human organization: Its management and value.* New York: McGraw-Hill.

O'Connell, S. (1979). *The manager as communicator.* New York: Harper and Row.

Peters, T.J., and Waterman, R.H., Jr. (1982). *In search of excellence: Lessons from America's best-run companies.* New York: Harper & Row.

Taylor, A. (1986, January). Part-time faculty: Properly using and not abusing. *Association for Communication Administration Bulletin,* 86–88.

Taylor, A. (1989). *Communicating.* Englewood Cliffs, NJ: Prentice–Hall.

CHAPTER 3

Communicating with Administrative Peers

Ronald L. Applbaum

8:00   Met with dean to discuss next year's departmental budget.

11:30   Brown bag with other chairs; informal discussion on strategy for next year's budget.

Isaac Stern, the violist, was once asked how any number of musicians could play the right notes in the right order, but only some made beautiful music while others did not. "The important thing is not the notes," he replied. "It's the intervals between the notes." In identifying the importance of the intervals or connections, his observation applies equally to the creation of "effective department administration" in academic institutions. A fundamental ingredient of "effective" administration is the connection — communication — between administrators.

The critical role of communication in the administrative process is stressed throughout this book. Each chapter looks at one or more components of the communication, often from diverse perspectives. Successful administrators — chairs, deans, vice presidents — recognize that their communicative actions are only a small part of the administrative process;

41

what creates "effective" communication is not their individual skills or specializations, but their interdependence. A limiting factor is the capacity to put the various skills and specializations *together* — to play the intervals as well as notes — to see and develop the interconnections between and within the institution's administrators.

In *Searching for Academic Excellence* (1986), Gilley et al. point out that the "efficient and harmonious functioning of an administration" is important in achieving institutional goals. Clearly, communication among administrators plays a major role in achieving institutional goals. Success is characterized by institutional teamwork and strong administrative teams. Gilley et al. (1986) found two basic administrative models for institutions on the move. The first consisted of administrators with complementary backgrounds, personalities working harmoniously, but with less intense team relationships. The second consisted of administrators with intense daily interactions, full involvement with each other professionally and individually capable of feeling for one another. However, in successful institutions, teamwork permeated the administrative hierarchies and administrator connections occurred across and between administrative levels.

Connections Among Administrators

Howard Bowen (1977) suggests that administrators "arrive at decisions by acquiring as much information or evidence as possible and then rely on informed judgment — a combination of sensitivity, logical inference and common sense" (p. 22).

Decisions by academic administrators come from integrating quantitative and qualitative information. Most administrators try to increase the amount of information they provide others when involved cooperatively in the decision-making process. They want other administrators to better understand their reasoning. Administrators also seek better informational bases for developing questions for solving problems.

Information is an essential ingredient in the administrative process. The specific informational needs vary by level — department (chair), college (dean), division (vice president) and institution (chief executive officer). In this chapter, I will focus on the communication between and among chairs, deans and vice presidents.

In general, as we go up administrative levels, we find the data needed become less specific. Department chairs need very specific data on day-to-day operations. For example, a chair routinely requires information on specific faculty members, students and course enrollments to make scheduling decisions. The dean needs more general enrollment information that applies across departments to make college scheduling decisions. Deans need workload trends and departmental enrollment patterns to determine planning goals and resource allocation. Vice presidents generally require fewer specifics on departmental or college operations, but not necessarily less information, to determine planning goals, policy guidelines and resource allocation for their division. For example, group data on enrollments, faculty and space utilization are needed to determine if institutional objectives are being met.

Administrative levels frequently differ in the time and control requirements of information. Frequently, vice presidents are bound by presidential request(s), governing board orders, state regulatory board guidelines and statutory requirements. In Texas, for example, public universities file over three hundred *different* informational reports each year with state agencies. While most of these are completed at the divisional level, many are sent to the college or department for completion, particularly for daily operational information. Many of the reports require discussion between deans or chairs to assure consistency in reporting.

Types of Interaction

The sharing of information between and among administrators falls into four basic interaction categories: (1) formal/structured, (2) formal/personal, (3) informal/structured, and (4) informal/personal. Formal relationships are defined by institutional structure. Administrative level tends to dictate the nature of formal relationships, while informal relationships are defined by personal preferences and informational needs.

Most academic administrative structures are seen as *formal and structured*, the traditional bureaucratic organizational model as discussed in chapter 1. The structure is hierarchical in that authority moves downward through a chain of command. Authority and "legal rationality" establish the rules of interaction, rather than friendship or personal loyalty. Communication follows established channels; it has a formal set of rules, regulations and record keeping practices. Most chairs and deans work within a relatively flat organizational structure, with few levels separating them; thus, more interaction occurs between chairs and deans than would in many businesses.

The budget process is a classic example of formal/structured interaction. Senior administrators establish procedures for preparing budgetary requests and communicating that information between levels. Budget preparation and discussion usually begin in the department and move up the bureaucratic structure. Formal hearings, involving chairs at the college level, and deans, at the divisional level, are common. Senior administrators often centralize the final decision — usually restricting chairs and deans from participating.

Interactions often become formal, rather than functional, communications between administrators. *Effective* communication is defined differently from formal and functional perspectives. For example, if a budget meeting is scheduled for chairs, the agenda published and only two of ten chairs participate, the formalist will say the chairs have been consulted. All policy and procedural requirements were met. The functionalist, on the other hand, will take the position that if only two of ten chairs met, the chairs were not consulted.

Fund raising events and planned retreats place administrators into *formal/personal* contexts. Interactions are less structured and more idiosyncratic. In such contexts, the topics might range from shop talk to small talk. However, the focus is still on the formal purpose behind the administrative gathering.

Informal meetings between administrators, informational networks and unscheduled conversations on task-related topics are *informal/structured* interactions. Administrators do not rely solely on formal/structured interaction for critical information needed to make decisions. Effective administrators go outside formal channels and use informal networks to acquire a picture of the total environment. The informal/structured interaction often takes on a mentoring relationship between administrators at different levels (e.g., chair and dean, dean and vice president).

Informal/personal interaction is characterized as a system of informal communication between professionals. The administrator's position does not determine who communicates with whom. Since these interactions are voluntary, they reflect the personal friendships among administrators from different administrative levels.

Academic Organizational Structure and Administrator Communication

In the Dr. Doolittle stories, there exists a Pushmi-Pullyou — an animal with a head at both ends, an animal impossible to tell whether it is coming or going. All academic administrators, but particularly department chairs, see themselves as this fabled creature.

At one end of the administrative chain, chairs are pushed by faculty, students and interested community members. At the other end, the CEO is pulled by a community that supports the institution to "produce" students who fit societal needs. And, throughout the institutional structure, each administrative component — chair, dean or vice president — feels pressure on their communicative connections.

In most institutions, administrators are caught in the "pushmi-pushyou" of centralizing or decentralizing decision-making processes. Administrative participation and communication varies considerably as a result of either decision-making format. The next section looks at the role and impact of participation on administrators.

Centralized/Decentralized Communication

Floyd (1985) identified campus-wide academic senates, a managerial orientation by administrators, collective bargaining agents for faculty and increasing power entrusted in system level personnel and statewide higher educational authorities, as factors leading to a trend of increased centralization.

In a centralized decision-making structure, participation is restricted. Chairs represent faculty and deans represent chairs. Typically neither chairs nor faculty have *direct* input to senior administrators. In times of major institutional crisis, fiscal exigency for example, institutions tend to further centralize decision-making and restrict communication among administrators.

Centralized decision-making is neither desirable nor feasible in all situations. Decentralization of decision-making at all levels — department, college, division — is often desirable for two reasons. First, increased communication among administrators increases overall administrative morale and satisfaction. It also provides a basis for greater feelings of involvement and commitment regarding decision-making. Second, participation reinforces the importance of an administrator's contribution and role in institutional operations and development.

Unfortunately, in the majority of cases, participation by chairs tends to reflect departmental and/or college provincialism, failing to consider critical institutional needs and goals. Communication among chairs or deans on institutional issues often aggravates a split between disciplines or colleges, making it difficult to implement or revise academic programs, course offerings or to foster interdisciplinary cooperation. Nevertheless, decentralization is often preferred by administrators because it leads to the type of interaction needed to produce short-term reduction for such potential conflict. Increasing administrator participation on issues and goals often leads to increased personal satisfaction and better job performance.

Direction of Communication

Communication direction — or flow upward, downward or horizontal — has relational implications. Here we look at the ramifications of communication direction associated when an administrator transmits or receives information. For example, as a president, I send messages (1) up, to the governing board and legislature; (2) down, to vice presidents, deans and chairs who report directly or indirectly to me; and (3) horizontally, to other presidents and CEO's.

Higher education is often viewed as an *authority pyramid*, where communication between administrative levels flows from superior to subordinate — CEO to vice president to dean to department chair. Today, the crucial role of downward communication among administrators remains unquestioned. The needed implementation of a more decentralized decision-making model on academic campuses has created a greater awareness of this necessity.

DOWNWARD COMMUNICATION

The most powerful factor affecting downward communication is institutional structure. Messages flowing downward tend to grow and change as they move through the hierarchy. The original message often is no more than a statement requiring action at a lower level. The dean and/or chair may add information specifying the means for achieving the desired results. By the time the original message (order for action) reaches the faculty who implement it, the order may be a fully detailed plan.

As one moves downward in any hierarchical structure, there is a dramatic reduction of information content. This *filtering* often leads to senior administrators being better informed than those at lower levels. So much information may be lost between a vice president's oral directive and the chair's receiving the message from a dean that the chair cannot understand the requirements for successfully completing the task. In such cases, filtering leads to role ambiguity and information inadequacy.

A lack of openness between or among administrators often distorts or blocks downward-directed information. A dean may transmit only the information necessary to accomplish a task and withhold information perceived irrelevant or potentially harmful. Few administrators communicate information that may damage them. Generally, *administrators only send messages that appear in their best interests.* The openness of one senior administrator may be affected by the openness of other administrators with whom they interact. Many administrators manage incoming messages by sorting out information not consistent with their perceived needs and interests. A chair may not listen to a dean calling for increased class sizes when his or her faculty are against larger enrollments.

UPWARD COMMUNICATION

In *Megatrends* (1982), John Naisbett noted a societal movement toward bottom-up, rather than trickle-down communication. As decentralization of decision-making processes in academic institutions increases, upward communication among administrators also increases. Most routine upward communications are related to the accomplishment of specific tasks under directives from the higher level administrator. However, upward communication often provides a picture of the problems, plans, accomplishments and feelings of lower level administrators. More importantly, such communication supplies critical information on the effectiveness of downward directives and institutional policies.

Message filtering also occurs in upward flow. Not surprisingly, the messages are normally positive in tone. Information about achievements are more often transmitted than information about mistakes or problems. There is a tendency for chairs, deans and vice presidents to withhold negative information from higher levels, particularly on personal and budgetary matters. Frequently, the lower level administrator distorts a message to conform to what he or she thinks senior administrators want to hear. However, upward communication often fosters greater trust, an important antecedent to administrator openness and accuracy. A chair is more likely to seek interaction with a trusted dean and to express satisfaction with their communication if the upward communication is effective. A lack of trust leads to information distortion, rumor and message ambiguity. Chairs who do not trust their deans often withhold information. Trust is such a critical factor in administrative communication that it may override any power or authority residing in the senior administrator.

Some administrators, even in a decentralized structure, do not view others as accepting listeners. Many topics become taboo and, therefore, are not discussed. While many low-level administrators believe they deserve a greater voice with senior administrators, particularly prior to decisions directly affecting them, most senior administrators fail to note their inaccessiblity. Generally, improving upward communication flow improves downward communication as well.

HORIZONTAL/LATERAL COMMUNICATION

Horizontal communication occurs among administrators at the same level. Decentralized decision-making has increased the flow of horizontal information, especially between departments. Chairs, deans and vice presidents meet regularly as separate consultative bodies to discuss issues of mutual concern. Academic councils often contain administrators from different levels who foster lateral communication among like-level administrators.

Horizontal communication among administrators performs several important functions. First, the formal and informal communication between department and school provide a basis for developing broader, more institutional (rather than narrow departmental or school) unit perspectives. Second, lateral communication provides a coordinating vehicle, maximizing productivity. Such coordination is essential for the setting of priorities within resource limitations or developing interdisciplinary programs. Third, it provides a basis for sharing information among administrators and enhancing task and socio-emotional effectiveness. Finally, administrators at all levels are often the targets of unwarranted as well as warranted charges and problems. Interaction among same-level administrators can serve an outlet for anxiety, frustration and fear.

Horizontal communication assists in coordinating departmental or college units in a division. In more autocratically administered institutions, senior administrators possess information about each college and/or department, but restrict that information from individual units. By withholding information from individual units, senior administrators increase their power and make lower level administrators dependent on vertical information channels.

As horizontal communication increases, it becomes more important for administrators to coordinate their interactions. Unrestricted horizontal communication often leads to increased conflict and misunderstanding, particularly on task-related issues. Chairs may restrict the amount of information they share with fellow chairs if they perceive a competition for limited resources. A desire for merit, promotion or recognition also makes chairs reluctant to communicate.

Academic Decision-Making and Administrators

Today, academic decision-making requires the participation and cooperation of faculty, students, community *and* administrators alike. Not all participants have an equal part in the decision-making process, however, and authority for final decisions must be delegated. Normally, final decisions are made by an academic administrator. Because of this, the legitimacy of the process becomes a question of trust on the part of *all* parties. For example, if faculty and administrators are involved in an adversarial relationship, information that is crucial to effective decision-making may be withheld by one or more parties. In this case, ability to control information yields power. Effective administrative communication is characterized by openness, trust and acceptance of legitimate authority.

Mortimer and Caruso (1984) have suggested that five things impact critically on openness and trust in academic decision-making: (1) early consultation, (2) joint formulation of procedures, (3) time to formulate responses, (4) availability of information and (5) adequate feedback. Let's see how these are applied to administrative communication.

1. *Early consultation.* Lower level administrators need an opportunity to develop alternatives and explore issues, prior to any narrowing of possible decisions. For example, if the budget process is truly open, input from chairs and deans is needed from the beginning as to budget parameters, constraints, priorities, etc.

2. *Joint formulation of procedures.* All participants should have an opportunity to develop the decision-making process for their academic unit. For example, deans might develop with their chairs the schedule and presentation format for budget hearings and the method for prioritizing budget requests from limited resources.

3. *Time to formulate responses.* Many administrators (particularly chairs) complain that their administrators (deans and vice presidents) give them insufficient time to react to or make decisions. For example, a vice president might allocate deans one month to prepare equipment priorities for an academic year. While this appears sufficient from the vice president's perspective, both deans and chairs must thoroughly consult with each other and faculty, which may take more than the allotted month. Chairs need sufficient time to explore their options and make reasoned, rather than rushed decisions.

4. *Availability of information.* Informational needs vary and some administrators restrict or filter information depending on the context and direction of communication. It is important that the appropriate level of information be provided by administrators. For example, during a budget presentation by a dean to a chair, the dean may withhold information that could cause conflict and call for a more equitable distribution of resources among departments. In doing so, the dean must be prepared to justify the restriction or lose the trust of the chair.

5. *Adequate feedback.* When an administrative decision is made at any level, it is important that the decision is communicated to all administrators participating in the decision *and* those impacted by it. For example, in establishing equipment priorities for a college, after discussion with chairs, the dean decides that office equipment should be given low priority. If the amount of equipment funds to the college is limited and there is no equipment allocation guarantee, chairs forwarding only requests for office equipment may not receive an allocation. The dean should have warned the chairs ahead of time that office equipment had a low priority.

Administrators are faced with a decision-making paradox. They must balance a desire and need to make decisions swiftly and decisively with a desire for openness and broadly-based participation. Earlier in this chapter, it was noted that many view academic institutions from a bureaucratic or rational model (Peters and Waterman, 1982). Such a model favors centralized decision-making because problems are defined and solved by the highest level administrator with little consultation at lower levels. This decision-making approach usually leads to a formal/structured interaction between administrators. Chairs will relate to deans and vice presidents according to strict organizational divisions. Typically, the chief academic officer maintains tight control over decisions. Even in daily operational matters, chairs are unlikely to take action without approval and are hesitant to make suggestions or offer information. For example, strict budget control is typical of an academic bureaucratic model. While a chair may be a department account manager, senior administrators require advance approval and often many forms must be completed and signed prior to use of the account. *The administrative emphasis in the bureaucratic model is on control, not communication.*

In the 1970s and 80s many institutions in severe fiscal trouble moved to greater centralized decision-making. In a period of fiscal austerity, centralized decision-making and planning are used to maintain or expand control over resource allocation. As resource conditions improve, restricted participation can cause confusion, conflict and frustration. It is difficult for a chair to work cooperatively without understanding the issues that must be addressed in planning and budget decisions. The absence of information about resource conditions leads to indifference or even conflict among administrators who view institutional decisions only from college or departmental perspectives. Indifference among administrators creates an unwillingness to work together. A lack of openness between chair and dean creates distrust, lowers morale and stiffles innovation and experimentation.

Department chairs are quite different from non-academic managers. Chairs are highly educated and often independent thinkers. Trained to be critical, they exhibit a great deal of skepticism regarding proposals. Most chairs have strong self-concepts and, thus, they have their own ideas about education, the department and the institution. Unfortunately, many academic institutions do not utilize the knowledge and skills of its administrators, faculty or students. To be more effective, recognizing the need to capitalize on the talents of all its people, academic institutions have moved toward a more participative model.

McCorkle and Archibald (1982) suggest:

> The critical decisions needed during uncertainty, such as setting priorities for resource use within programs and between programs, determining when curricula need to be renovated or dismantled, and planning the most effective array of faculty talents, cannot be established effectively from on high. Rather than "Do this and that," the operating principle must be "Do whatever is necessary to achieve agreed-on objectives effectively and efficiently." This management principle provides extensive freedom for department chairs and other managers to act relatively independently within plans, policies and delegations of authority. (p. 111)

The participation model is characterized by open communication, delegation and acceptance of responsibility, broad involvement in policy formulation and rewards for successful accomplishment of administrative duties and responsibilities. This model assumes that administrators are more enthusiastic, productive, satisfied and creative when they take an active part in making decisions that affect them.

This decentralized model focuses on administrator inter-action as a critical element in decision-making. It calls for administrators who listen to others and have trust and confidence in them. Moomaw (1984) has developed five prin-ciples of participative academic leadership that apply to administrative communication:

> *Articulating Mission and Goals.* A common problem in academia is that administrators, as well as faculty, are often unclear about institutional mission and goals. Adminis-trators need to discuss and know their institution's role and scope and institutional priorities need to be known. The chair needs to know the programmatic priority of his or her department in relation to other departments in the college and institution. Continual communication and planning among administrators can keep them focused on long-term objectives, rather than short-term problems.

> *Developing Leadership Teams.* In *Searching for Academic Excellence* (1982), Gilley et al. reported that all up and coming institutions instituted effective leadership teams. Administrator interaction was successful in pro-viding the basis for cooperation, information exchange and experimentation. These teams often delegated daily opera-tional details to specific team members. For example, most institutions have a formal consultative group composed of chief academic officers. The group might be delegated responsibility by the vice president and CEO to develop institutional policy regarding general education. Such groups are instrumental in making decisions impacting long-term planning. One member of the group, the Dean of Arts & Sciences for instance, might be delegated respon-sibility for operational oversight of an implemented general education program. In turn, the chair in communication would be delegated responsibility for oversight, that is, scheduling, staffing and advising his or her department's course requirements in the general education program.

> *Encouraging Broad Involvement in New Ideas.* To para-phrase Moomaw (1984), the ideal administrator is one who, upon seeing another administrator fall after sawing off the

wrong end of a tree limb, would help the other to his or her feet and compliment their innovative spirit, encouraging experimentation. *Encouraging ideas isn't costly and it builds support for making future changes.* While implementing new ideas such as programs can be costly, program acceptance and allocation of limited resources may be more acceptable if administrators have been involved in the discussion and development of the new program proposal. For example, the Communications chair at the University of Texas-Pan American was unable to gain a commitment for a new faculty position from his dean until he discussed with him future programmatic needs and goals.

Evaluating. All administrators are involved in an ongoing assessment of personnel and programs. In academic affairs, the sharing of ideas on how the review takes place is critical in establishing equity in the evaluation process. Chairs need to know how their colleagues are evaluating their own faculty, particularly in respect to tenure and promotion decisions. Since personnel evaluation problems tend to be similar across departments, the sharing of information among chairs clarifies and strengthens the evaluation process, reducing future problems. Unfortunately, chairs and deans avoid discussing evaluation problems, because many administrators view them as reflecting negatively on their leadership. However, in an open climate, a trusting relationship can be built and chairs may safely share evaluation concerns.

Using a Reward System. Administrators, like faculty, need to be motivated to work hard for the institution. Personal satisfaction and altruistic motives of chairs are not sufficient for sustained performance. Feedback should be solicited from administrative peers to ascertain one's level of perceived performance.

Administrators recognize that a completely decentralized, democratic form of decision-making involving all administrators is neither practical nor effective for all decisions. Effective administration requires the administrator to know which activities to centralize and which to decentralize. Generally, as we move down the hierarchical structure, administrators decentralize routine activities, planning for implementing institutional goals and resolving unit problems. A vice president does not arrange course schedules for a particular department. In contrast, the establishment of an institution's mission, role, scope and master plan are concerns of senior administrators. Most institutions follow a loose-tight principle; that is, the co-existence of a firm central direction when necessary and maximum individual autonomy when possible.

Summary

Major change in academia occurs slowly. Many administrators resist change because of negative prior experience and/or they fear the consequences of more, improved or effective communication. Others are reluctant to divest centralized power. Some do not believe in the value of change until they have experienced it. A small number will not want to share the decision-making responsibilities needed to improve communication.

Improving communication between academic administrators is not self-executing. Administrators have to make it work, and to make it work they have to understand the total communication process as it operates at their institutions. Higher education's need for improved administrative communication remains as perennial as its need for constant change in response to society's needs. Academic administrators must examine their connections with all other administrators. Constant reflection and fearless criticism are the price for effectively functioning administrative communication.

The forces transforming us into "pushmi-pushyou" creatures never cease. A chair must understand and accept the impossibility to administer the department successfully. However, one should not underestimate the importance of effective communication among administrators in meeting one's respective duties, responsibilities and solving problems.

References

Bowen, H.R. (1977). *Investment in learning: The individual and social value of American higher education.* San Francisco: Jossey-Bass, Inc.

Floyd, C.E. (1985). *Faculty participation in decision making.* Washington, DC: ASHE.

Gilley, J.W., Fulmer, K.A., and Reithlingshoefer, S.J. (1986). *Searching for academic excellence.* New York: ACE/Macmillan Publishing Co.

McCorkle, C.O. and Archibald, S.O. (1982). *Management and leadership in higher education.* San Francisco: Jossey-Bass, Inc.

Moomaw, W.E. (1984). Participatory leadership strategy. In D.G. Brown (Ed.), *Leadership roles of chief academic officers* (New Directions in Higher Education, No. 47, pp. 19–30). San Francisco: Jossey-Bass, Inc.

Mortimer, K.P., and Caruso, A.C. (1984). The process of academic goverance and the painful choices of the 1980s. In D.G. Brown (Ed.), *Leaderhip roles of chief academic officers* (New Directions in Higher Education, No. 47, pp. 43–48). San Francisco: Jossey-Bass, Inc.

Naisbett, J. (1982). *Megatrends.* New York: Warner Books.

Peters, T., and Waterman, R.H. (1982). *In search of excellence: Lessons from America's best run companies.* New York: Harper & Row.

CHAPTER 4

Managing Grievances

Fred E. Jandt
John A. Kaufman

3:45   Met with departmental tenure and promotion committee to review guidelines.

4:30   Met with students in Intro class about possible sexual harassment by instructor.

Some people yearn for the professional life found in *Goodbye Mr. Chips*, where faculty devoted their lives to students and unseen administrators somehow kept buildings open. In this academic community, students, faculty and administrators all worked together devoted to truth and learning. Conflicts — when they arose — were dealt with through logic and reasoning in the belief that a truth could be discovered that all would accept.

Some faculty view themselves as independent scholars in the pursuit of knowledge. As knowledge "entrepreneurs" they view other work (teaching, committee work, research) as a necessity, permitting them to do what they "really want to do." Conflicts that usually arise involve others who have impeded their life's work; resolution is sought that permits them to continue this work.

Few faculty see themselves as laborers with defined performance expectations in a highly structured and centralized bureaucracy. Images of assembly-line factory workers do not easily replace images of Mr. Chips. But academia is rapidly becoming more a bureaucracy and less a community of scholars. *This change is altering the role of the department chair, the relationship between chairs and faculty and the way conflicts are resolved.* Bureaucracies are often sources of conflict, requiring more formalized procedures for resolving disputes once settled informally. Concurrent with the change to bureaucracy, other external factors affect how conflicts are resolved, including organizations such as the American Association of University Professors (AAUP) and labor unions.

External Policies Impacting on Grievance Procedures

Chairs must be familiar with both internal and external grievance policy. Internal policy is often found in the administrative and/or faculty handbook. This policy, however, is often influenced by external policies that address due process and grievance procedures.

AAUP (American Association of University Professors)

Since its founding in 1915, the AAUP has been concerned with due process and grievance procedures. Its policies are published in the AAUP Bulletin and compiled in periodical AAUP Policy Documents and Reports. Three statements particularly relevant to chairs are the 1958 statement on faculty dismissal proceedings, the 1971 statement on retention of faculty appointments and the 1976 statement on academic freedom and tenure. Litigants often cite these policies to support their cases. Whether or not AAUP policies are officially adopted, they often provide a frame of reference for defining academic freedom, tenure and due process.

An important AAUP document, "Declaration of Principles," proposed procedures for dismissal. This document identifies three basic elements of due process: (1) charges should be in writing and "formulated with reasonable definiteness," (2) there should be a fair trial before a "special or permanent judicial committee chosen by the faculty senate or council, or by the faculty at large," and (3) faculty should have "full opportunity to present evidence," with adequate provision for expert testimony if one's competence is at issue.

Typical AAUP grievance procedures require a hearing by a faculty committee. Testimony, evidence and briefs are allowable, and the committee transmits its decision to both the administration and the grievant in writing. Normally, the administration accepts the faculty committee's decision. Under AAUP guidelines, only after receiving the committee's decision can a final decision on the grievance be made.

Collective Bargaining Agreements

The grievance procedure is a systematic review of contract violation complaints. Grievance arbitration, as a means of resolving disputes, is "part and parcel" of the collective bargaining process in both the public and private sectors.

Industry developed grievance systems after the 1935 National Labor Relations Act. Not until the 1960s, however, were substantial numbers of academic institutions covered by collective bargaining laws. Cutbacks in resources and declining student enrollments led to the corresponding growth of grievance systems. Faculty unionism and collective bargaining emerged as dynamic forces on both public and private campuses. Collective bargaining and grievance arbitration redefined the role of the department chair, calling into question the concepts of *collegiality* and *shared authority*.

Further, arbitration continues to spread beyond the confines of contract violations. Student and faculty disputes over areas not covered in collective bargaining contracts, as well as faculty disputes on campuses without collective bargaining agreements, are frequently resolved through grievance procedures. For example, at Northeastern University, where no union or collective bargaining agreement exists, a grievance is defined as:

a complaint by a faculty member that he [sic] (1) Has been discriminated against on the basis of age, sex, race, religion, national origin, or marital status, (2) Has been denied academic freedom, (3) Has been dismissed without just cause, (4) Has been denied due process in consideration for tenure, renewal of contract, or promotion, (5) Has been subject to a violation, misinterpretation or inequitable application of provisions of the Faculty Handbook, or (6) Has otherwise been treated unfairly or inequitably.

With the use of grievance procedures increasing, it is safe to assume that both faculty and administration rely more on legal processes. The trend is to systematized deliberations and increased sensitivity to due process concerns. Clearly, the collegial model of resolving conflicts no longer prevails.

Areas of Grievances

Chairs routinely operate in an environment of potential conflict situations. Relations with other chairs, deans, senior administrators, union representatives, students, part-time and full-time faculty, support staff, outside vendors and parents, if not managed, are capable of producing conflict and formal complaints. Chairs should consider faculty and students as significant *potential* areas of conflict. Regardless of the party or the circumstance, chairs should attempt to defuse potentially volatile situations early and informally. Chairs, whether acting as judge, mediator or chaplain, should always encourage *informal* settlement of disputes.

Student Grievances

Student grievances often relate to one of four issues: (1) admission to degree programs, (2) academic advisement, (3) grade appeals and (4) disciplinary action. In each area, the chair's role is to informally prevent or successfully arbitrate the dispute.

ADMISSIONS

In our experience, problems relating to admissions disputes stem from ambiguous admission requirements, preferential interpretation of requirements or absence of formal appeal procedures. Chairs of over-subscribed programs seeking to limit majors should expect more admissions disputes than chairs in departments with growth potential.

Potential conflicts in undergraduate programs increase when non-majors take departmental courses but are subsequently refused admission to the degree program. This situation can be prevented if chairs instruct their faculty to explain at the beginning of each term that course enrollment does not guarantee admission to the program. Although disclaimers usually result in lost FTE (full-time equivalents), an oversubscribed program's losses are usually insignificant.

Graduate students enrolled before acceptance frequently cause conflict for the chair, whose mercy and approval they inevitably seek. The scene is familiar: A student enrolls as an "at-large" student, pending application and acceptance to a specific degree program. Under at-large status they can take several departmental courses. The dispute occurs when the student is subsequently denied admission. Such disputes can be minimized by (1) making certain that faculty, in class and during advisement, inform students of the program requirements; and (2) enacting a formal appeal procedure, one that is recognized and publicized. Appeal procedures actually reduce the number of grievances. For instance, a national survey of graduate programs in social work showed that, while applicants who appeal often have decisions reversed, programs offering formal appeal procedures have relatively few appeals.

ADVISING

Advising disputes usually occur *ex post facto*, after students suddenly discover obstacles standing in their way. The most common complaint is that a student was misadvised about graduation requirements. Initially, students place the blame on the advisement procedure or on a particular advisor. Chairs often find themselves playing the role of ombudsman, receiving a complaint for which they are expected to suggest courses of action. Chairs need to listen with both an empathic and analytic ear. Empathic listening creates an impression that they are concerned and genuinely interested in solving the problem. Analytic listening is important in ascertaining the facts, so the student can be advised of available options. It is also important to review both the facts and the procedures to ensure that erroneous advisement is not the actual cause of the problem.

GRADE APPEALS

Grade appeals almost always require the chair to become a referee, as student and faculty argue over the propriety of a course grade. Appeals create highly charged emotional climates. Students and faculty usually approach appeals hearings from a *win-lose* perspective. The situation creates circumstances that are a real test of a chair's communication skills and leadership.

Before the chair referees a grade dispute, however, it often helps to first assume a chaplain's role. In our experience, chairs are almost always approached *after* an initial, informal attempt to change the instructor's mind has failed. Once again, this is an occasion for empathic listening. Clues in the student's conversation often provide a deeper understanding of the real cause of the complaint. Perhaps personal circumstances prevented the student from obtaining the grade he or she was capable of. The grade at issue might simply be a symptom of an unrecognized problem (family responsibilities, work, social interactions, illness, unrecognized learning disabilities, etc.) in the student's life. A good listener can gently probe into the student's circumstances, discovering that the grade complaint masks a serious problem adversely affecting academic performance. Empathic listening may eliminate a potential grade dispute by focusing the student on the real cause(s) of substandard performance. Sometimes, however, a *formal hearing* is the only resolution for the dispute.

Most institutions have prescribed administrative procedures for hearing grade appeals. Once an appeal has been filed, the chair's first responsibility is to study the appeal procedure. If the institution's legal staff has not been notified of the appeal, this is the time to do so. This indicates that an appeal has been filed and that the chair may be calling for interpretations of rules or for clarification of procedure. Once the chair is familiar with the appeals procedure, which normally incorporates a hearing, he or she needs to make sure both student and faculty understand procedural guidelines and are aware of their responsibilities. At this time the chair should review the rules of evidence, as specified in the appeals guidelines. If students are allowed advisors at hearings, they should be informed of their role in the process and, especially, during hearings. Some institutions permit advisors to comment during hearings, others limit advisors to communication with only the student during the hearing. The chair's communication role at this stage is simply informational, but the function is important to ensure an orderly and efficient hearing. These actions and precautions go a long way in encouraging professional conduct during the hearing.

Most institutions' grade appeal procedures create an appeals committee and designate the department chair as its presiding officer. To ensure fairness and integrity to the proceeding, chairs must be thoroughly familiar with the hearing's procedures. *New chairs should talk with experienced chairs who have taken students and faculty through the process to gain insight and appreciate some of the nuances that come only from experience.*

Hearings proceed best if the official instructions are read and the function of the committee, standards of evidence and responsibilities of participants are reviewed. Once presentation of evidence has started, chairs are required to keep the proceeding on track: keeping the discussion focused on the primary issues and watching for diversions into examination of motive. All parties should stick to the facts as presented.

Questions put to the chair during the hearing should be answered with precision and certainty. If a chair is not certain about an answer, a recess or postponement is appropriate and the institution's legal staff asked to provide an answer to the question. Thoughtless or tentative answers confuse the hearing process or even render outcomes invalid. The chair should take the participants through all the steps specified for a hearing. Upon conclusion, the chair should thank all participants and inform them how and when the committee's decision will be communicated.

DISCIPLINARY ACTION

The chair's role in a student disciplinary action is similar to that in a grade appeal. However, the stakes are higher in a disciplinary action. Sanctions can range from oral reprimands to outright dismissal from the institution. In most cases, formal judicial review boards outside of departmental jurisdiction handle disciplinary actions. Consequently, a chair may not be a facilitator; nevertheless, if a faculty member brings a complaint against a student, the chair is brought into the dispute immediately.

As with grade appeals, the chair should try to work out an informal solution to the conflict. As mediator, he or she establishes the factual situation by separately interviewing the student and faculty or staff members making the complaint. If the situation can be resolved informally, the chair should decide on a remedy and present it individually to the accuser. If the remedy is mutually acceptable, a follow-up meeting of conciliation between the parties should be held to confirm the resolution of the dispute.

Faculty Grievances

Faculty grievances usually involve sexual harassment, academic freedom, tenure and promotion, merit pay, workload or discriminatory treatment. The chair needs to understand the various communication roles and responsibilities he or she has with various types of faculty grievances. The chair must be well-versed in procedural matters and cognizant of the resources and services available to assist in dispute resolution. Services and facilities vary, but most institutions have an ombudsman, affirmative action officer or personnel officer to provide support and services in dispute resolution.

SEXUAL HARASSMENT

Sexual harassment is generally defined as unwelcome sexual advances, requests for sexual favors or related verbal or physical contact interfering with a person's performance or creation of an intimidating, hostile or offensive work environment. (See the Equal Employment Opportunity Commission's *Guidelines on Sexual Harassment*.) Students, faculty and staff are potential targets of sexual harassment. The American Council on Education has noted that academic institutions are morally obligated to develop policies shielding students and employees from sexual harassment.

The chair's responsibilities in sexual harassment cases are twofold. First, *the chair must inform and educate faculty and staff about the institution's sexual harassment policy and its provisions*. Prescribed disciplinary actions that can result from rule violation should be discussed. This includes making faculty and staff aware of the behavior or language that construes sexual harassment. Generally, sexual harassment takes on several forms: (1) trading sexual favors for evaluations or grades; (2) repeated or flagrant sexual advances; (3) demeaning verbal or nonverbal communication in instructional *or* noninstructional settings. Most institutions have lists of behaviors judged as sexually harassing. The chair should reiterate them to faculty and staff. Sexual harassment policy should be discussed with new faculty and reviewed annually during a faculty meeting. To create awareness and acknowledgement, the information should be communicated both orally and in writing.

The chair's second responsibility is to *counsel students and employees who believe they are being harassed*. Often behaviors not seen by one person as capable of creating an offensive work or school environment are, in fact, perceived by another as expressed sexual harassment. "Perceived" is a key work in the equation.

Many times complaintants prefer the chair to handle the situation by informally telling the faculty or staff member that an informal sexual harassment complaint has been received. At this stage chairs have two responsibilities. First, a specific description of the offending behavior must be obtained. Second, the chair must discuss whether the plaintiff wishes to be identified; this is often a judgment call. Most formal grievance policies do not allow the anonymous charging of sexual harassment. However, when informally resolving a *potential* harassment situation, it often facilitates the process and secures compliance if the complaintant's identity is not disclosed. In such a case, a suggestion to the accused that some misunderstanding has occurred but, nevertheless, as chair, you are concerned and take *all* such charges seriously. This is a good time to reiterate institutional sexual harassment policy, an approach that clearly signals that the person's behavior has been challenged, yet affords him or her an opportunity to affirm institutional policy without admitting guilt. Normally, this technique puts an end to the problem situation.

If harassment continues, an official investigation is necessary. In such instances, the chair first informs the complaintant of the procedure for filing an official complaint and initiating an investigation. Chairs involved in either formal or informal proceedings should keep a *precise written record* of all discussions regarding the case. The chair will be called to testify once a committee has started to collect evidence and listen to testimony. Remember, regardless of feelings for or against the parties involved, chairs must carefully protect the privacy and confidentiality of all proceedings, formal or informal.*

ACADEMIC FREEDOM

Academic freedom infringement is an area of faculty dispute that puts chairs on guard and makes daily communication awkward. Several practices facilitate communication and, if all goes well, understanding under such circumstances.

A chair should know what constitutes "academic freedom." If not, check how the institution has administratively defined the term. It is important that both chairs and faculty understand what principles define academic freedom — and in what context. If no statement exists, the AAUP's academic freedom and tenure statement offers guidelines. The statement includes the following provisions, paraphrased here:

1. Faculty are entitled to full freedom in research and publication of findings. Compensated research should be conducted based upon institutional consent.

2. Faculty are entitled to freedom in classroom discussion but should not include controversial matter having no relation to the subject. Limitations imposed due to religious or other institutional aims should be clearly stated in writing.
3. When a faculty member speaks or writes as a citizen, he or she should be free from institutional censorship or discipline. However, faculty should be accurate, respect the opinions of others and not present themselves as official spokespersons.

Although these and similar statements on academic freedom are painted broadly, they provide guidelines gauging whether specific pedagogical instructions or directives could violate academic freedom. Academic freedom is more complicated, of course, for private institutions that construe academic freedom within some religious or secularly-defined paradigm.

TENURE AND PROMOTION

Disputes involving tenure and promotion are more likely to appear on a chair's agenda than violation of academic freedom charges. The chair's role in tenure and promotion cases is a function of his or her part in the performance review process. In some institutions, chairs do not recommend candidates for tenure or promotion; they simply provide descriptive information about the faculty member's teaching assignments, committee work, community service and professional development activities. In such cases, the chair's communication in a grievance procedure is usually limited to clarification.

However, if the chair has responsibility for performance evaluation, as well as describing responsibilities and activities, he or she plays a more crucial role in the grievance process. A chair recommending against tenure or promotion is naturally perceived by the faculty member as an antagonist. Recommending a faculty member turned down at later levels of review places the chair in a more positive light. In either case, administration and the grievant expect the chair to play the roles they perceive as *appropriate to the circumstance.*

How the resolution process affects the professional relationships between a chair and the faculty is determined by the grievant's definition of the chair's role. If the chair evaluates faculty performance, his or her assessment may be cited by the grievant as unreasonable or capricious. Such circumstances foster an adversarial relationship. It is important to isolate the grievance issue from daily communications with the faculty member — no easy task given the circumstances.

OTHER GRIEVANCES

When a grievance centers on issues related to work load, scheduling, work conditions or discriminatory treatment, chairs are almost always portrayed in a formal grievance as the offender. In such cases, whether a chair has performance evaluation responsibilities is of little consequence, the grievant often perceives the injury as stemming directly from administrative treatment. Once again, the preceding admonition applies: *Try to keep all communication respecting the dispute to the actual grievance forum and keep daily communications with the faculty member as dispassionate as possible.* This requires a great amount of self-control on both the chair's and grievant's part, but it is the only professional course of action to follow.

The Grievance Process

Academic chairs are first-level managers. As such, they are often targets of complaints because employees — faculty, staff, and their unions — use management as a scapegoat for their own professional shortcomings. *Chairs should understand that formal grievance procedures are a part of the job.* Instead of viewing them as adversarial proceedings, antagonistic by nature and disruptive by design, chairs should look at three positive effects of grievance resolution.

First, a formalized grievance procedure permits interpretation of contract provisions without work disruption.

Informal attempts at resolving disputes are often inadequate for negotiating agreements where the parties are diametrically opposed on important issues. Second, a grievance procedure can be cathartic, purging work-related anxieties and lowering stress. Third, a formalized grievance procedure helps managers to detect labor problems early, before they seriously impede obtainment of departmental objectives.

Grievances typically evolve around five basic elements: (1) definition of grievance, (2) definition of grievant, (3) procedural steps, (4) procedural limitations and (5) neutral, third-party participation.

Definition of Grievance

Unions and employee organizations try to establish a broad, all-encompassing definition of matters that can be formally grieved. Administrators, not surprisingly, try to establish more situation-specific definitions of grievable actions. Four grievance definitions are in general use today: broad, narrow, compromise and special limitations. *Broad definitions* — favored by unions and employee organizations — include anything that affects employees in the work place. A *narrow definition* confines the grievance process to negotiated items, such as maximum teaching load per term. Management prefers the narrow definition, which is legalistic in its execution; however, most grievance definitions in use are of the compromise type, hybrids of broad and narrow definitions. Under the *compromise definition,* specific provisions of the master contract can be at issue, as well as management actions perceived by employees as adversely affecting their working conditions. *Special limitation definitions* incorporate language that reserves specific prerogatives to management, such as removing from grievance issues relating to assignment of supervisory personnel.

As noted, once a grievance has been filed by a departmental employee and the disputed action defined, chairs should have a good understanding of (1) their role in the procedure; and (2) the information to be communicated during the process. For instance, a chair recommending against tenure, along with senior administrative reviewers, will be

defined by the grievant as a "perpetrator." If a chair recom-
mends for tenure, but senior administrators turn down the
faculty member's request for tenure, the chair might be
perceived by the grievant as an ally. *As a manager, the chair
still has his or her fiduciary obligation to the institution.*

DEFINITION OF GRIEVANT

Usually, we tend to think of individuals as being the
grievant in formal dispute resolution. However, institutions
may operate — through negotiated agreement with a union
— from a broad definition of "grievant," one allowing either
an individual or an employee association to file a complaint.
Chairs must understand what definitions of grievant are used
at their institutions. If an employee association files a
grievance for actions that are within the chair's administrative jurisdiction, he or she may be placed in a situation
requiring more time and energy than if the action were
simply the result of an individual faculty member's filing.

Procedural Steps

Procedural steps for processing a complaint, the third
element in grievance resolution, are usually precisely defined
and must be followed to the letter of the law by both sides
to ensure a valid resolution. Procedural steps can vary
significantly from institution to institution, but most provide
for a two-level hearing process. At the first level the grievant
seeks *informal* resolution with his or her supervisor, which
in an academic department is usually the chair. If the
complaint cannot be satisfactorily resolved through informal
procedures, then the grievant moves to the second level, writes
a *formal complaint* and files it with the campus personnel
office. After the complaint has been received, the case is
scheduled for review before a hearing committee. The hearing
committee may be a standing committee, but typically is an
ad hoc committee convened solely to hear evidence related
to the complaint. Normally, institutional handbooks contain
procedural rules which guide grievance hearings. Once the
committee has reviewed the evidence and heard arguments,

it makes a finding and forwards a recommendation for final review, often to the office of the president.

Procedural Limits

All grievances are conducted within prescribed procedural limitations, the fourth element in the grievance process. Limitations usually speak to time limits for filing and answering a complaint, the role of employee representatives in the process, formats for documentation and filings and issues respecting confidentiality.

Third-Party Review

Third-party neutral review of a grievance allows the process to transcend the innate political relationship between management and employees or their unions, an often acrimonious relationship limiting the usefulness of the grievance process. Third-party reviews either involve advisory arbitration or binding arbitration. *Advisory arbitration* involves further fact-finding, culminating with a recommendation. Advisory arbitration is just that, advisory. Its value is found in the facts and logic the arbitrator brings together in the recommendation. *Binding arbitration* mandates that both institution and employee accept the finding of the arbitrator as a substitute for their judgment.

Approaches to the Grievance Procedure

Although these elements are universal in the grievance process, several different management approaches — or attitudes — to the procedure are possible. The three most common are the "literal contract" approach, the "human relations" approach and the "moderate" — or "compromise" — approach. The chair's role during a grievance is influenced by the institutions approach to the process.

The *literal contract* approach is legalistic. It reflects a management attitude of constant vigilance against unionism or third-party encroachment of its prerogatives. Grievances, under this approach, officially interpret contract language in dispute by parties bound to a master contract.

The *human relations* approach regards the master contract as a general outline of responsibility. Grievances are seen as forums through which both employee and management refine and re-interpret responsibilities and obligations. This approach adopts a "safety valve" metaphor in describing its purpose. Employee grievances are seen as potential *warnings* that something is amiss and a mid-course correction is in order, an approach compatible to a philosophy of participatory management. Institutions operating more from bureaucratic than collegial models do not emphasize the humans relations approach.

The *moderate approach* to grievances is, as its alternative name implies, a compromise between the legalistic and human relations approaches. Theoretically, it draws on the best attributes of each. Management's attitude is one of willingness to abide by arbitration of disputes relating to major contract provisions directly impacting an employee — merit pay, promotions, working conditions — while protecting its rights respecting allocation of resources, planning and goal setting. Generally speaking, the moderate attitude toward negotiated settlement is predominant in academia.

Compatibility between grievance approach and the institution's managerial philosophy is crucial to any successful grievance process. An administration with no master agreement, but taking a literal attitude to grievance resolution, undoubtedly creates confusion and resentment in the process. Obviously, a human relations or moderate approach is more conducive to a successful grievance process. Chairs must understand these dynamics to participate in any grievance process intelligently and usefully.

Review

The chair's attitude and role in the formal grievance proceeding is determined by two basic factors. First, of course, is the institution's managerial attitude toward the grievance process. Although chairs are first-level managers, they may be a member of the collective bargaining unit. This puts a chair in a difficult position, perceived as neither fish nor fowl in the eyes of the grievant *or* senior management. Chairs who are not bargaining unit members will be expected to approach the grievance from management's perspective. Superiors insist on this and, in most cases, the grievant expects it also.

The second factor shaping the chair's role in a grievance is the grievant's definition of the chair's relationship to him or her. A chair may be cast as a perpetrator, ally or expert witness by the grievant. If the defined role is incongruent with the situation, the chair must explain to all involved how he or she can add clarity to the grievance process. For instance, chairs may be mandated only to describe faculty members areas of responsibility, they may be prohibited from offering an evaluation of performance. The chair's role in grievance cases involving denial of tenure or promotion, then, is largely defined by jurisdictional boundary. A faculty member who has filed a grievance after being refused promotion might expect his or her chair to become a staunch ally in the procedure when, in fact, the chair cannot play that role.

Recommendations for Chairs

Whether an institution employs a broad definition of grievance, one that permits a hearing of any employee complaint, or a limiting, narrowly drawn definition, chairs, as first-line managers are likely to be the first people communicated to about a complaint. Experience shows that initial reaction to a complaint is the most critical dimension in the grievance process. In many cases, chairs are in the best position to prevent a complaint from escalating into a formal grievance. Chairs are also positioned to prevent potential complaints by recognizing situations within their jurisdiction that might precipitate a complaint. We think chairs can work to prevent complaints or, failing that approach, resolve them early and informally by observing the following six guidelines.

First, *remember that grievance resolution is one of the chair's primary responsibilities*. Chairs are obligated to meet with dissatisfied faculty and staff to discuss any circumstances that might contribute to a problem. Chairs are also obligated to follow the prescribed institutional procedural guidelines sincerely and in a reasonable manner.

Second, *do not treat a complaint as a personal attack.* Once the issue has been brought to the chair's attention, it should be examined objectively. It is more productive to seek clarification when communicating with a potential grievant. No one expects chairs to be infallible, but they do expect them to be concerned and responsive. The problem should be discussed at a meeting quickly set up and at a time mutually agreeable to all parties. The chair should make certain that no interruptions or other distractions occur during the time set aside for the meeting. People seldom feel that they have received a fair hearing if the secretary interrupts or fails to hold telephone calls. Chairs should give the grievant their undivided attention.

Communication is a two-way street, so a chair should give all parties close attention and *listen actively* to their stories. Chairs should avoid trying to second guess where the stories are going and mentally developing counterarguments as others speak. The best approach is to stay calm, be objective and, whatever the nature of the complaint, do not resort to "fighting words": "misinformed," "special treatment," "ignorant." The chair should pursue a descriptive line of questioning. For example, "What aspect of next semester's teaching schedule do you feel is unfair to you?" will lead to greater clarification than noting "You're not being treated any differently from other faculty in the department."

Chairs need to obtain as much relevant, factual information as possible from the meeting. Effective chairs look for a particular solution or alternative courses of action that might remedy the situation, to include suggestions from the grievant. A good strategy is to paraphrase aloud the situation and complaint as described by the employee. The chair might ask him or her if the situation was presented accurately. This technique often verifies the situation as perceived by the grievant. But, more positively, it might serve to downgrade the urgency of the complaint. The chair should keep in mind that grievants have indulged in intense personal feelings before the meeting, agonizing over the severity of the situation and rehearsing in their minds the confrontational scene with the chair. Sometimes amazing things happen when communication switches from the personal to interpersonal; the additional context adds new meaning and perspective. A chair employing this strategy should not be astounded if, after hearing the complaint paraphrased, the grievant retreats from his or her original position, acknowledging that perhaps the situation is not quite as critical as first thought.

A chair should not discount the value of an apology in resolving complaints. Sometimes an apology from the chair is enough to stop a festering resentment from ballooning into a formal grievance. An apology is not an admission of guilt or wrongdoing, but simply acknowledgement that a particular situation is causing dissatisfaction for the person, which the chair regrets.

Third, follow Harry Truman's favorite motto and *do not directly blame a higher authority. The buck stops with the chair.* A chair may not personally agree with policies promulgated at higher levels, but he or she is responsible for following them and explaining their relevance to faculty and staff. If a complaint centers on the chair's actions or policies, he or she needs to carefully consider why and decide whether the complaint has validity. If it does, and the chair decides to correct the conflict, he or she should consider communicating the decision to make the change to all affected. The confidentiality of the person who originally voiced the complaint, of course, must be maintained.

Fourth, *do not take a grievance as a mark of personal failure.* A good chair, making tough decisions, is bound to create some situations that result in individual dissatisfaction and lead to a formal grievance. In fact, an absence of complaints may indicate that something is wrong. The National Association for Education suggests that something might be amiss if the unit has never had a grievance filed against its policies. Complaints are a natural byproduct of decision-making. Other chairs have faced similar situations; a little collegial shoptalk can do wonders for a chair's confidence level.

Fifth, *respond to all complaints in a timely manner.* If the situation calls for the chair to investigate, establish a time frame for the investigation. Although many chairs are inclined to do so, the matter should be not put off. If required, while maintaining the employee's confidentiality, the chair should do some fact checking and discuss the situation with peers and superiors. If a master agreement specifies procedural time lines for disposition, the chair must follow them.

Once the assessment is completed, the chair should meet with the employee to review the situation. If the complaint and remedy are justified, do so with equanimity, thank him or her for calling attention to the problem. If the complaint is disallowed, the chair should provide a careful, thorough justification for the decision. The chair must inform the employee of all the considerations that went into the decision; explaining the decision's reasoning both orally and in writing. The written statement should be concise and less involved than the oral explanation. Chairs with reputations for fair, prompt action on complaints, typically are successful at resolving disputes informally.

Sixth, as chair of an academic department, *have in place a crisis management plan.* Crisis management plans usually have three components: a liabilities inventory, a list of tools and expertise available to manage crises and procedural guidelines to guide action during a crisis.

A *liabilities inventory* is simply a list of problems or situations that have the potential to precipitate a crisis. By crisis, we mean an unstable but crucial time for an organization when decisive change is pending. A liabilities inventory helps identify those potential situations, and, possibly, to prevent them. One of the best ways to compile a liabilities inventory is to look at the history of grievance cases filed. The personnel office can help with this. Although privacy laws do not allow grievance files to be opened to administrators at large, someone in personnel can describe the types of grievances, their situations and frequency that are part of the institution's history. The chair can then juxtapose what's reflected in the grievance history with the existing departmental situation. Is anything going on that seems to rhyme with the circumstances reflected in a former grievance situation? If so, the chair can prepare some preventive measures.

Lists of resources available for use should include the names of personnel who have special expertise or standing in the institution. For instance, is there an ombudsman to assist in dispute resolution? What sort of jurisdiction does he or she have? How successful has he or she been in resolving complaints. Ombudsmen have been working on American campuses for years, but their individual franchises and roles vary from institution to institution. The chair should be on the alert for "unofficial" ombudsmen, faculty or staff who can serve informally to resolve complaints. Many departments have one or two senior faculty who naturally fall into mentoring roles with junior faculty. Chairs should recognize and enlist them to keep the department functioning. Additionally, the chair should acquire copies of master agreements, faculty handbooks and pertinent documentation promulgated by the institution about how negotiated agreements are implemented.

Procedural guidelines, the third component in a crisis management plan, should suggest various grievance strategies available. Generally, these are of two types: those that can used informally and those that are officially mandated by a master agreement. Chairs should keep thorough notes of all grievance activities, describing actions taken in particular incidents, lines of reasoning employed, possible remedies, reaction of plaintiffs, successful negotiations and so forth. Many chairs use this information to create their own personal "crisis management procedures manual." Before beginning, however, it is a good idea to sit down with the administrator responsible for grievances and learn what strategies and procedures have worked in the past.

Summary

This chapter has examined the chair's role in a variety of grievance situations. All chairs deal with conflict. Not all conflict can be resolved through informal discussion. Some conflict inevitably will evolve into a formalized grievance.

Knowing how grievances differ, the institution's policy regarding grievances and the procedures to be followed make the best of an uncomfortable situation. Finally, six guidelines for efficient grievance management — crisis management — were suggested.

---

*The American Council on Education publishes an excellent short report of its recommendations for combating sexual harassment. For a copy, write to it at One Dupont Circle, Washington, DC, 20036.

CHAPTER 5

The Budget Process

June Kable

9:30 Met with dean to discuss department's needs for next fiscal year.

3:00 Faculty meeting — appraise faculty of the "state of the department" and next year's funding forecast.

The budgetary process is a complex persuasive communication act. This process of persuasion covers a time frame of many months, and the chair acts as both persuader and persuadee throughout. The budgetary process is ominous, mystical and often the most intimidating aspect of the new chair's responsibilities. It is the most important persuasive act in which the chair is involved; it sets precedents, provides opportunities for growth, establishes credibility for the chair and makes possible the realization of departmental goals.

Any experienced chair knows the complexities of preparing for the budget process and often approaches it with trepidation. The focus here, however, will be on the new chair. Although there are many different types of accounting procedures as there are institutions, the approach here is more general.

This chapter addresses this complex process, along with its persuasive implications through the discussion of three suppositions: (1) *The mission of the institution provides the basis for communication and decision-making*; (2) *the administration is a persuasive audience which must be analyzed*; (3) *the faculty needs to understand the budgetary process.*

Mission of the Institution

Every budget request must be measured and assessed according to the institution's mission. The stated mission is usually found in the policy manual or some other institution-wide document. Researching past allocations provides new chairs with an indication of how this mission is articulated in the funding process. Specific facts of importance to discover include faculty-student ratios by department and alternative sources of funding (grants, gifts, endowments, etc.). This information indicates if the institution is primarily research-oriented or if the emphasis is on the liberal arts or technical programs, such as health sciences or pharmacy. Against this background of information concerning the mission, and therefore institutional priorities, a chair formulates a request that appropriately fits the institution's overall budgetary picture and mission.

Consistent with assessment of the institution's mission is the chair's need to know how much funding his or her department generates, thereby contributing to the fulfilling of the institution's mission. This information can be favorably compared to present faculty salaries and departmental operating expense funding. The chair should research other institutions' budgets of comparable size and similar missions. Additionally, if data from disciplinary associations are available, they, too, should be analyzed. *It is the chair's responsibility to educate the administration,* and the only way to do so is *with objective facts, supported by numbers.*

A new chair needs to discover how senior administrators (1) perceive the department; and (2) see its function in relation to the institution's mission. With this information as a base, it is then time to plan a persuasive strategy for the budget process as it relates to both the administration and the faculty.

The Administration

When assessing the administration, it is important to realize that deans and vice presidents are compelled to play a "numbers game." Their credibility is dependent on the record of faculty-student ratios, valid justifications for expenditures and an image of making fair and equitable monetary decisions for all departments and divisions under their umbrella. Further, other chairs must be considered. Today's economy often creates a competition for limited resources. New chairs often enter the budget process with an "I win/You lose" attitude. However, with time, new chairs learn to work with other chairs to get their allotted budget. United fronts among chairs often persuade the dean that the chairs' needs are his or her needs, too.

Deans

With this understanding of the senior administrator's needs, the chair should prepare his or her budget request. Normally, the chair presents his or her budget to the dean. In preparing the budget several things are evident. Both the program and faculty needs, usually philosophical in nature, should be translated into quantitative justifications in preparing for the dean's presentation. *It is also important to provide the dean with alternatives.* Using "if-then" reasoning, a chair might state that "If we are unable to fund 'a' *and* 'b,' then would it be possible to fund 'a' from the budget and pursue funding 'b' from an alternative source?" (Sources such as private funds, administration funds or institutional grants, if available.)

Chairs usually address departmental budgetary needs in a private meeting with their dean. First, in preparing for this meeting, chairs should create back-up documentation for all budget requests. It is to the chair's advantage to include well-organized and concise work sheets with brief item justifications, along with any required documents. This preparation becomes the basis for arguments for departmental needs during the budget meeting. It also serves as a working document that the dean can use for reference at a later time in the institution's budget process (e.g., the dean's presentation to the vice president).

Chairs need to "trouble-shoot" or project needs for the future. If equipment is dated, replacement requests should be made before it becomes unworkable or obsolete. Effective chairs, through reoccurring assessment, alert their deans a year or two before the expenditure needs to occur. As a result, the dean and chair can plan future equipment expenditures in an orderly fashion. The dean's need to be forewarned is also fulfilled. During regular meetings with the dean, it is wise to discuss future goals of the department and the projected costs to realize them. Doing so includes the dean early in the planning process. This provides the chair with information on how and when to make requests and allows the dean to make suggestions and offer advice. When the items appear on the official budget request, the dean is already informed and, more importantly, is involved.

Some chairs adhere to the philosophy of "Ask for more than the department needs to get what you really need." This procedure is often effective for a year or two. However, when the dean catches on, the chair loses his or her credibility and the department suffers as a result.

When a dean refuses a budget request, the chair must rely on alternatives prepared for such an occasion. For example, suppose the dean refuses to grant the funding for adjunct faculty necessary to meet projected enrollments. An argument from "residues" works well here by providing alternatives:

> If we don't receive funding we could (a) delete "x" number of sections, with the resultant decrease of "x" credit hour production; or (b) we could enroll 40–50 students in each section, but we can no longer support individualized instruction; or (c) we could increase existing faculty members' loads, which would effectively eliminate their scholarly productivity. Since these are our alternatives, how do you suggest we resolve this issue?

A dean's needs are for impressive numbers in student enrollment, for performance, laboratory and seminar courses that are not compromised and for his or her faculty to be productive scholars. Chances are, because the chair's alternatives do not meet these needs, the request for funding most (if not all) of the necessary number of adjunct faculty will be approved. By preparing alternative arguments, the mutual fulfillment of needs on the part of both the dean and the chair can be met.

It is crucial that the chair know what is important to the dean. What are his or her needs? How are these needs articulated into priorities? What is the dean's perception of his or her role within the framework of the institution's mission? Answers to these questions provide a framework for the chair's communication strategy in persuasive interactions related to the budget process.

The Faculty

Faculty members often do not understand the budgetary process. Most new chairs are former faculty members who quickly become aware of their previous lack of understanding of the intricacies involved in preparing and presenting a budget. Chairs often approach communicating about budgetary matters with the faculty from two extremes. First, they may keep the entire process to themselves. Or, second, they may try to over-involve them in the process. Both extremes are unworkable.

It is imperative, however, that faculty members have input into the budget process. They are the chair's primary source of information. Effective chairs seek such input in several ways. First, each faculty member might present to the chair his or her needs, specifications and justifications in writing. This preliminary step prevents faculty from submitting "wish lists." Second, the chair should discuss each faculty member's request with him or her. This step provides possible alternative arguments for later use *and* affords the chair an opportunity to informally discuss goals, as well as reviewing faculty progress during the year. From these private discussions, the chair sets his or her own priorities.

In discussions with each faculty member, the chair becomes aware of the needs of each as a persuadee. When he or she believes that a faculty member's request is unreasonable, given budgetary constraints, mission or administrative priorities, choices and options must be presented to the faculty member. Suppose a faculty member requests $35,000 worth of laboratory equipment. The chair, as the faculty member's administrator, knows that a $35,000 request will be denied. The chair's persuasive strategy should be similar to that used with the dean, the chair should offer alternatives solutions. In this case:

> Since the cost is so prohibitive that the request will be denied, why don't you look into the possibility of a lease/purchase agreement? I believe the administration would find this solution palatable and you would get your equipment. OR, I like your idea and think that it has merit. But, given this year's budget, we need to look at other funding sources. Have you checked out XYZ Corporation? They often help acquiring — or partially underwriting — equipment in your area. Maybe we could go to the dean with a partial request, if the corporation would fund the rest.

This interaction is an example of an interactive-dependency approach to persuasion. The faculty member wants laboratory equipment. The chair wants a solution that the dean would find acceptable. Effective persuasion occurs when a solution is found that mutually satisfies the needs of all involved.

At each faculty meeting the chair should include the budget process as an agenda item. Because the budget process covers a period of many months, campus-wide rumors tend to develop. If, for example, the legislature is in the throes of decision-making concerning higher education funding, reports of it often appear in local and campus newspapers. *The chair must keep the faculty appraised of the true situation as it is known at that time.* The situation is often misconstrued by faculty reading newspapers without an understanding of the *entire* budget process. For example, if the papers announce that faculty will receive a seven percent raise, the chair must explain that the increase is seven percent over the total amount allocated to faculty raises in the previous year. Faculty must understand that the figure includes not only monies for across the board raises, but also for merit increases, salary adjustments and promotions; therefore, while most faculty will receive some salary increase, there will not be an automatic seven percent raise for everyone.

Faculty members often do not understand that there must be a spirit of reciprocity between faculty and administration. The dichotomy between administration and faculty is often expressed in the rhetoric of "them versus us." This attitude is reflected in statements such as, "The administration *should* give our department higher salaries, more funding for travel or more operating funds."

The chair's best strategy is to educate his or her faculty about budgeting. This process often diffuses the "us versus them" syndrome and inculcates a philosophy of "If we perform well as individuals and as a department, we will earn the respect of the administration and be rewarded accordingly. If we accomplish 'a,' we shall have no difficulty in being funded adequately for 'b.' " The earlier laboratory equipment example is a good case. The faculty member may need to engage in a pilot study that can be used to indicate how effective the additional equipment might be in meeting instructional and/or scholarly needs, as well as the institution's mission.

Faculty members lack patience when it comes to the budget. It is to the chair's advantage to share with the faculty the various strategies he or she uses to reach departmental goals. *Patience is not merely a virtue, it is a necessity when engaging in the budgetary process.* Faculty have a hard time learning this lesson. They learn by observing their chair exercising patience and by observing that the end-result is the realization of the chair's and the department's goals. Often faculty members begin to use the same processes in their appeals to the chair. Of course, not all faculty respond positively. Each chair has his or her share of "nay sayers," faculty who never understand nor adapt to the behaviors necessary to facilitate departmental goals. *Faculty should also understand that the process of persuasion is not always successful.* Sometimes a chair loses a small issue only to come back and win a larger one later. While the chair tends to look at the overall department, faculty often see just one issue.

And, finally, *all communication with the faculty concerning budget requests must articulate the institution's mission*. Many faculty are so concerned about their own discipline that they lose sight of the institution's overall goals. Therefore, it is the chair's responsibility to articulate this mission and the department's place in it.

Summary

New chairs have an advantage over new administrators in other departments when they understand that the process of persuasion is effective only if the needs of both persuader and persuadee are fulfilled. New chairs must also understand the need to be credible with both the dean and the faculty. Persuasion is the most effective "tool of the trade" a chair possesses.

Preparing a budget and persuasively articulating it to administration and faculty is a time-consuming process. Understanding and articulating the institution's mission in budget allocations is a necessary part of the chair's assessment of the current and future situation. Understanding the needs and desires of senior administrators and the necessity to fulfill those needs provides additional information for the chair's assessment. The faculty also have needs to be fulfilled, but they must understand both the process and the psychological environment in which their requests are perceived.

The new chair must learn and remember, as have chairs before them, that success is not always the result of persuasive communication. When a failure to persuade occurs, chairs should understand why and not lose faith in the process. Charles Henry Woolbert stated it best in 1920 when he wrote,

To study persuasion is to study human nature minutely. Without a guide to men's [sic] action probabilities, without appreciating and understanding their action grooves, a speaker or writer works in a vacuum and so has no possible means for insuring success. . . . More than half of success in winning men is in understanding how they work.

References

Woolbert, C.H. (1920). *The fundamentals of speech: A behavioristic study of the underlying principles of speaking and reading* New York: Harper & Brothers.

CHAPTER 6

Assessing Faculty

Robert M. Smith

8:45   Met with Professor Duncan to assess performance,
       re: research.

4:00   Faculty meeting. Assess departmental planning for
       next year.

*"We should all be obligated to appear before a board
every five years, and justify our existence . . . on pain
of liquidation."*
                                    — George Bernard Shaw

Faculty assessment is the consummation of a chair's
leadership efforts. One of my favorite deans believes that a
leader helps others achieve what they did not think possible
for themselves. From this perspective, successful leadership
is properly viewed through the accomplishments of the faculty
and is a direct reflection on the chair's communication skills:
the ability to articulate a vision for the department, the adept-
ness to persuade faculty to attain challenging goals consistent with the vision, and the capability to express a mutually
agreed evaluation of the endeavor.

Assessment requires a plan. Therefore, this chapter
presumes that planning and evaluating are part of a contin-

uing process. In this process, the chair takes on several communication roles: facilitator, negotiator, coach and evaluator.
This chapter examines the faculty assessment process in four
related stages: (1) *facilitating* a systematic plan for conducting
planning and assessment; (2) *negotiating* achievable faculty
goals; (3) *coaching* performance; and (4) *evaluating* the final
product or activities. A successful assessment process is
dependent on equally successful communication tasks by the
chair within each stage.

The chair's communication roles are not easy to fulfill.
There are many stumbling blocks to successful planning and
assessment. Chairs are often frustrated by the complications
that academic institutions add. For example, a chair might
have several problems present at one time: A faculty with
their own agenda of professional goals which may or may not
have been compatible with the institution's mission; And
faculty members believing strongly that they are independent of administrative dictates and personnel practices typical
of a regular business. This may be further complicated by
the fact that the chair is often elected for a fixed term,
creating a reluctance for conducting assertive assessments
knowing that he or she might revert to a peer relationship.

Importance of Conducting Effective Assessment

Assessment, or faculty evaluation, is an important leadership function of administration. Most institutions have in
place some formalized system for conducting faculty assessments and making it a matter of record. All too often, this
is a superficial assessment, simply satisfying administrative
requirements for a completed form. Assessment can be a
powerful tool, moving departments toward important goals
and faculty toward professional achievement. Some chairs
complete the assignment but miss making a meaningful contribution to their faculty and department.

Even when assessment is less than a careful and comprehensive design, it should be an important factor in development. For example, evaluation as part of a rigorous tenure

and promotion review process often provides a singular decision about a person: up or out. In the 1960s and 70s, with a relative abundance of faculty competing for available positions, academic institutions did not worry about the subtleties of developing faculty. Replacements for nontenured faculty were readily available.

Several trends in the past decade have increased the importance of well-executed assessment procedures by administrators. A shortage of qualified faculty is apparent. Personnel policies and practices are subject to legal review. At least a half-dozen federal laws specifically apply to hiring and firing faculty. The propensity for an aggrieved faculty member to litigate has made many administrators more cautious and defensive when assessing faculty performance.

The faculty handbook, once a congenial pastoral document describing idealized expectations and benefits of faculty life, has become a contract with great attention given to specific wording. No chairperson or faculty evaluator at any level should begin an assessment without having carefully read their faculty handbook. The most recent trend is an increased emphasis on "outcome assessment" measures. These techniques, rapidly being adopted by governing boards and regional accreditation agencies, place pressure on institutions to demonstrate to some external review body measurable gains of knowledge and skills occurring in the classroom. Few, if any, faculty are prepared to deal with the evaluation complications arising from this trend.

Assessment Functions

The unmistakable result of these trends is that higher education is moving to an increased emphasis on faculty assessment practices. These are inextricably tied to other departmental functions and have more to do with a department's success than any other chair activity. The ability of chairs to conduct *effective* assessment processes focuses on four assessment functions.

First, *assessment helps faculty attend to goals.* Assessment of faculty activities keeps the focus on long-term individual goals. Most faculty have experienced the exasperation of looking back over a period of time only to find that daily activities have taken them away from their goals. Long-term and complex projects often suffer unless faculty are sufficiently self-disciplined to stick to the task. Assessment helps safeguard faculty from drifting from important goals, making them more productive and valuable contributors to the department.

Second, *assessment establishes a progressive record of accomplishments.* Most chairs view the tenure and promotion process as based on a series of systematic achievements. Erratic activity or a sudden burst of productivity immediately prior to tenure or promotion review is usually viewed as suspect. Committees find annual reviews and records of assessment particularly useful in evaluating candidates. If the performance of the candidate is consistent, progressive and reflects stable productivity, the committee has more confidence that these behaviors will continue through the candidate's career. Annual assessments may be the only consistent evidence available to help the committee make an informed decision.

Third, *assessment promotes continuing communication with faculty.* Most faculty would not receive performance feedback or meaningful communication about their work if assessment was not required. Our research with administrators found that evaluation was one of the least-liked aspects of a chair's job. No wonder so many assessment sessions last less than one-half hour. Yet, the same research demonstrated that performance feedback was one of the most highly sought topics of communication by faculty and staff.

Fourth, *assessment offers renewal opportunities for senior faculty.* One of the most persistent questions raised by chairs is how to assure that senior faculty remain active and responsive to curriculum demands? A well-defined assessment plan, with defined evaluation stages, is a successful method for assuring renewal and change. The importance of communicating a chair's expectations to the faculty cannot be understated. When institutions change focus or when student demographic shifts cause program changes, faculty need to adapt and remain responsive to new conditions. How chairs communicate the need for adaptation, articulate new expectations and lead faculty through the change determines the department's future.

Facilitating a Systematic Department Plan

This chapter assumes a model of planning and assessment that takes into account emerging trends, fulfills the functions described above and realistically responds to the pressures chairs feel when conducting an assessment. The model is a repeating cycle of the activities of planning, implementing and assessing. Planning begins at least one year before the assessment and runs on a yearly cycle. During the mid-cycle stage the chair and faculty work together to achieve the plan. This stage includes intermediate adjustments of both plan and activities. The final stage is the assessment of achievements. The assessment leads into the plans for the *next* iteration of the cycle, which begins another full rotation.

The model requires the chair to demonstrate leadership through successful communication strategies. For the cycle to operate, however, the model must be accepted by the faculty. The following three sections describe characteristics of the model.

Facilitate Full Faculty Involvement

In academic institutions, the prevailing mood is to include faculty in design decisions made at each step of the assessment process. Even if it were otherwise, the smart chair wants those who are being evaluated to participate in designing and defining what should be evaluated. Faculty who have input into the process are more likely to accept it as fair and equitable. This provides the chair more communication strategies to make the assessment successful.

Developing the assessment process is often delegated to a faculty subgroup who report their recommendations to the faculty. If this method is used, the group needs to decide how the department's planned process integrates with the institution's structures, such as the tenure and promotion criteria specified in the faculty handbook. The assessment process has to successfully develop tenure-eligible or promotable candidates. It must also support other institutional documents, strategies, and policies.

Facilitate Acceptable Performance Categories

The institutional mission dictates on *what* criteria faculty should be assessed. Most often the categories of teaching, research and service organize an assessment plan. As a pervasive part of the academic vocabulary, teaching, research and service are often slurred together as one phrase. Twenty years of research indicates no change in the importance of these categories in assessing faculty performance.

The American Council on Education reports that, over the past decade, several common factors are used in faculty evaluation. The top seven factors are: (1) classroom teaching, (2) student advising, (3) campus committee work, (4) research, (5) publication, (6) public service and (7) personal attributes. Although institutions rank the order differently, the items appear in some form or another in most assessment plans.

Facilitate Assessment of MEANINGFUL Performance

The listing of items is not the focus of assessment. Lists are simply labels. For example, "research" means nothing in assessment without recognizable standards. The department must pursue "activity" or "outcome" assessment. Evaluation of *activities* is generally based on whether a faculty member participated in an event. Common events include conducting class, advising students, publishing research or attending committee meetings. *Outcomes* are products of activities. Did learning take place in the classroom? Were students advised correctly? Were there contributions made in committee sessions?

THE PREFERRED EVALUATION CHOICE IS OUTCOME ASSESSMENT.

Outcomes more closely relate to institutional and/or individual goals. The assessment is more functional and relevant when based on outcomes rather than listings of activities. However, it is difficult for chairs and faculty to present and evaluate *acceptable* evidence that demonstrates the actual outcome. Faculty are suspicious of outcome assessment, unless the plan clearly specifies how the data are acquired and evaluated. Consequently, chairs must be patient when working with faculty at this stage. Patience often leads to outcome assessment methods that produce reasonable expectations.

Facilitate Recognition of Departmental and Individual Needs

Finally, the department should base faculty assessment on a plan that helps the faculty member and the department as a whole achieve their goals. Planning and assessment should harness faculty energy to accomplish the mission of the department. Too often faculty become entrepreneurs, whose work is more prescribed to individual career or financial goals, not to advancing departmental goals. Ideally, chair and faculty should establish departmental goals and a set of strategies for achieving them. Good departmental planning includes a faculty accepting personal responsibility for achieving some dimension of each goal, even if that means setting aside some personal achievements. For example, after the faculty adopts an annual departmental plan, the chair should distribute it to each faculty member, and ask each to accept responsibility for specific goals in the plan. Most of the time, goals are shared, and some goals become part of everyone's responsibility.

Finally, the faculty should formally adopt the agreed upon assessment process as a governance decision. It is important that the faculty feel that they have had a chance to discuss and vote on the actual plan as it is to be implemented. This often bonds the faculty to the plan and later disagreements about definition or the weighting of individual items are easier for the chair to arbitrate.

Negotiate Goals for a Successful Work Period

Following the establishment of a departmental plan, the chair begins working with each faculty member on individual goals. These conversations produce tasks for the coming year that move faculty toward achieving professional development and contribute to the department's growth. The chair's communication role becomes that of a negotiator between what constitutes realistic and challenging goals and a faculty member's performance. The challenge is persuading the faculty member that these goals are worth accomplishing.

Negotiate Realistic Goals

Two opposite problems often develop with faculty goals: the overachiever and the underachiever. With the former, a chair simply helps the faculty member pare down planned activities to meet realistic expectations. A few projects performed well is better than many mediocre projects.

Underachievers present a more difficult case. Often a chair must set criteria for the underachiever's goals as the minimum level acceptable for a minimum salary increment or as satisfactory progress toward tenure and/or promotion. This precludes faculty from receiving a significant salary increase or being considered for tenure and/or promotion, unless they elevate their performance accordingly. Often these criteria take a cycle or two before change is observed. However, establishing *fair and achievable evaluation criteria* affords the chair the power to create change.

A third potential problem may occur with a new faculty member. This is a critical negotiation because it establishes behavior likely to last for years. A chair should take special care in presenting the planning session as a serious yet exciting opportunity for new faculty. The chair must set achievable goals, assuring that the new faculty member feels an opportunity to establish a successful faculty-chair relationship. If unsure of what performance to expect, a chair should err on the side of generosity. Such cases, however, require a mid-term review to possibly update and modify the agreed upon plan. This gives both a chance to build a productive relationship.

Negotiate Recognizable Evidence of Achievement

Part of any planning meeting is developing what constitutes acceptable recognition of achievement. A chair who establishes from the beginning what evidence demonstrates achievement solves many potential problems later concerning "acceptable achievement." Chairs may find it best to have faculty members come to the planning session with their own stated goals and criteria for achievement.

The selection of assessment goals is shaped by realistic choices defined by available evidence. Choices should present clear-cut information about performance. The measurement of outcomes depends on the evidence acceptable to establish an outcome criterion. For example, if a department decides that research publication is a relevant category, the various levels of publication that define success must be decided. Many times, this is translated into publishing in refereed journals. In an outcome assessment model, the achievements are often defined in *successive levels*, where each level awards a different value based on significance. For example, articles in a regional journal would have some value, national journal of greater value and in a leading national journal of highest value. Outcome assessment might include how often the research is cited by others or the research being identified as seminal in the discipline.

When the same analysis is applied to teaching, providing unambiguous evidence of quality teaching becomes an elusive task. Institutions often employ a combination of indicators. Although one midwestern university actually lists 101 ways to evaluate classroom teaching, the American Council on Education suggests that most teaching assessments are based on systematic student ratings and the chair's evaluation.

In any case, a chair — in conjunction with the faculty — needs to decide both how and what constitutes evidence of quality teaching. The trick is in evaluating the evidence. For example, are student ratings to be compared to a set of criteria, a norm established by other faculty or previous levels established by the faculty member? Two conditions are quickly evident. First, *multiple sources of evidence are more desirable than single sources*. Simply put, the more ways a chair can document the quality of faculty productivity (research, teaching, service), the better the assessment process. The latest survey of assessment practices clearly indicates a trend toward broad-based assessment. As many as four different sources is not uncommon for determining teaching competence.

Second, *a series of progressive assessment decisions with different values awarded for each level of achievement are more desirable than a single level.* This hierarchical arrangement must be developed carefully and with significant faculty input. A chair should expect disagreement during this stage of development. His or her most difficult task is keeping faculty open to realistic but challenging goals. Again, care should be taken to avoid setting levels easily achievable but not sufficiently challenging.

A faculty planning and assessment model that specifies the steps to be followed, and both the criteria and the performance indicators necessary for satisfying the criteria, makes the chairs' job much easier. The critical factor in achieving this is negotiating acceptable and reasonable goals with the faculty.

Coach Performance During the Work Period

The process of assessment is a continuous set of communication activities. Our research in faculty evaluation suggests that if the process is not formally mandated by the institution, evaluation probably would not occur. Yet, the same survey suggests that most faculty expect and want more (rather than less) feedback on their academic performance. Chairs need to take a more positive view of faculty development arising from planning and assessing. For that reason, the term "coaching" is appropriate when examining the chair's role at this stage of assessment. Like the metaphor developed in chapter 1, a coach not only leads, but develops the skills of his or her players, often becoming a private tutor to individual players. A coach is an active participant before, during and after the sports event. In contrast, the "evaluator" remains passive and enters the process only at the end, usually too late to make a difference in performance.

Ideally, the communication between a chair and his or her faculty is so pervasive that, when formal assessments are made, there are no surprises to either party. This requires continuous faculty-chair interaction.

To achieve continuous feedback, a chair might build in special mid-year review sessions with faculty. Due to budget cycles, many institutions conduct annual faculty reviews in January or February, so that salary recommendations can be formalized before the end of the fiscal year. This cycle requires that faculty build their plans to carry through half of the next year. A logical mid-year review comes at the beginning of the fall term, when both the department and chair are tooling up for the forthcoming term. The mid-year review helps faculty review progress, adjust goals to accommodate circumstances that have developed since the formal assessment and re-emphasize goal-directed activities.

The nature of the chair's feedback is equally important throughout the year. Sessions, whether formal or informal, should target one or two areas for comment. A sharp focus on priorities is much better than asking faculty members to keep track of multiple projects. The chair must keep in mind, however, that faculty members have these projects in process. Therefore, the communication strategy is to work on *action* steps that assure completion of the project. This is a time for encouragement and mapping strategies for accomplishing the task, not evaluation. If no progress occurs, then a chair may suggest breaking tasks into more defined segments, with deadlines for each. Most people work well with reasonable deadlines.

Part of the chair's job is defining how to support faculty members. One of the compelling aspects of this metaphor is that the coach is not the star, but helps the players to score points. Therefore, the coach role is supporting, cultivating, stimulating and encouraging of faculty performance. Chairs help identify resources, schedule courses and activities and run interference in ways that assure the faculty achieve their goals. For a chair to discover faculty member needs, continuous feedback is as important as is monitoring their progress.

Coaching Special Cases

Part of the feedback process is discovering problems or special performance cases. Although other chapters address this more directly, it is worth stating that dealing with problem performance cases are part of the assessment process. Experience suggests that most, if not all, of the difficult personnel problems faced by chairs are due to the absence of feedback. I cannot recall any case resulting from too much communication.

The general adage for dealing with special performance cases is: "Take care of the molehills and the mountains will take care of themselves." Prompt feedback and frank, focused discussions when problems first develop are great cures. Coaches call timeouts to enable the team or an individual to settle down before resuming a game. However, many chairs seem to assume that problems will self-correct and go away as the game is played. By waiting until the end of the year or when the game is over, he or she has already lost.

Time *sometimes* helps clarify and develop perspectives, but often it leads to entrenched habits and other deep-seated difficulties. An intervention review should be held as promptly as possible when a special assessment case arises. The focus should be on the incident or performance problem. The session should begin with a description of what is happening (or not happening) followed by an opportunity for response by the faculty member. This response is important because a chair has his or her own perceptions of an event or series of events. The faculty member may have an entirely different perception. Both need to understand the differences in their views. Therefore, a chair should probe the faculty member's view and listen to how he or she interprets events or activities.

Depending on the response, the chair may suggest specific corrective action. A set of deadlines or milestones for the proposed activity is important. However, the key to this process is that follow-up assessments be specified and enforced. Otherwise, the corrective plan may appear as merely a bluff on the chair's part. Chairs should be sure to write a brief note about the incident, a reminder of the agreed plan and the follow-up procedure. (Documentation is a tricky part of the process and involves legal questions. As noted in chapter 4, chairs should carefully review institutional policy and procedures on personnel actions, especially those regarding corrective actions.)

The importance of communication during this stage of the assessment process cannot be overstated. Feedback within the context of the helpful and encouraging coach metaphor sets a climate that encourages success.

Evaluate

The final step in the assessment process is evaluating faculty performance. Although chapter 7 focuses on the *appraisal interview* in detail, a quick overview of its relation to the assessment process helps round out this chapter's discussion.

If the assessment plan were clearly articulated with unambiguous standards for performance and frequent interactions in the interim, the evaluation step is a comfortable part of the assessment cycle. The final assessment should be a productive extension of the chair's relationship to the faculty. Anxiety often occurs when there is fear of the unknown, a fear that can be eliminated through continuous feedback. Anger, which occurs when there is perceived unfairness, or frustration from unwarranted criticism can be eliminated through preparation and concentrated attention on the needs, goals and perceptions of the faculty member.

Several pitfalls can develop in the final assessment session that merit mention. Evaluation research reveals that at least two debilitating factors often enter the final assessment: halo and recency effects. The *halo effect* occurs when an evaluator lets some positive aspect (the "halo") of the individual's performance overrule all other aspects of his or her performance. To compensate, the chair should carefully prepare a list of the performance areas under review, giving weight to all performance areas identified earlier in the planning sessions.

Recency effects occur when the chair considers only the last few days or weeks of the performance under review and generalizes this to the entire year's performance. Recency is overcome by having a record of the entire year's performance in the faculty member's file. Depending on memory or anecdotal scraps leads to an uneven and potentially unfair assessment of the individual's performance.

The actual meeting should be planned with a clear understanding of what areas need to be discussed. The session should focus on how the faculty member's performance relates to his or her earlier plans and how it leads to continued growth and development. The chair should also prepare options for any necessary corrective action. A successful session leaves the faculty member with the impression that the chair is helpful and sincere and that the chair has made a credible review and assessment of his or her strengths and weaknesses.

Following a mutual discussion of performance, the chair should discuss the next planning cycle. The assessment should be a continuing part of the model built in this chapter. *Therefore, assessment is really a temporary benchmark along a growth plan.* The assessment is like a road map. The chair's communication defines the clarity of available paths and signals confidence that this is the correct path.

Following the session, chairs should prepare a written record of the assessment, give copies to the faculty member for his or her review and file it in the faculty member's permanent records. For the process to continue, the chair must allow the faculty to review and even offer corrective information on the written assessment. Many institutions require the faculty to certify that the assessment fairly reflects the evaluation period. If the faculty member believes that it does not, he or she may offer in writing his or her perception and both become part of the official file.

Summary

The important consideration for chairs while working with faculty is that they are influencing careers, affecting disciplines and shaping institutions. They make choices and

have the power to exercise them in ways that make a difference. Departmental, as well as faculty, leadership emerges
through successful communication. The chair's greatest job
and greatest accomplishments come from the achievements
of others. To communicate a sense of vision for the department, a belief in the ability of the faculty and an expectation of their performance creates an atmosphere where faculty
demonstrate their acceptance of the chair's messages through
commitment to quality performance. *The evaluation that
results is as much an assessment of the chair's skills as it is
of the faculty's.* Taken from that perspective, there is sufficient
challenge to communicate and to communicate well.

CHAPTER 7

The Performance Interview: Guidelines for Academic Department Chairs

Michael Stano

11:00 Appraisal interview with Professor Jones.

1:00   Developmental interview with secretary.

Performance appraisal interviews are used to evaluate and improve the performance of employees. As was pointed out in earlier chapters, department chairs in academic settings routinely assess the performance of their faculty to help them develop realistic goals for future work efforts. Performance appraisal plays an important role in retention, salary and promotion decisions.

Chapter 6 in this book presented a model for evaluation based on a cycle of planning, implementing and assessing. The principles discussed in that chapter reflect the assessment plan. The focus of this chapter is on preparing for and conducting the appraisal interview, the session where the chair formally evaluates and discusses performance with each faculty member. As noted in chapter 6, the appraisal interview is a natural part of an ongoing departmental assessment plan.

Unfortunately, appraisal interviews are often fraught with anxiety, hostility and defensiveness. Interviews with faculty who receive the highest possible evaluations are easy. Interviews with faculty who receive something less than one hundred percent ratings are often difficult for both the chair and the faculty member. Most chairs dislike communicating bad news; most faculty feel threatened and put down by negative evaluations. Thus, the relationship between the chair and the faculty is frequently damaged or destroyed during an appraisal. This creates an evaluation process that is commonly resented and often resisted by all involved.

Compared to academic chairs, most business professionals are better prepared to deal with the pressures of evaluation which are not so alien to them. In addition, the academic environment is normally much more positive and supportive than most business environments, yet academic evaluation is inherently critical and threatening. Unlike the chair, the businessperson is trained to conduct appraisal interviews. Finally, while the business literature is filled with information on appraisal, little has been published on the subject for academic administrators.

The purpose of this chapter is to make the appraisal interview more productive and to discuss problem areas so they are less traumatic for both the chair and the faculty. To examine the appraisal process, the chapter develops ten guidelines that chairs should follow in preparing and conducting the appraisal interview. Although this chapter focuses on appraisal interviews involving chairs and faculty, the guidelines are equally applicable to all appraisal interviews in academic settings. That is, the guidelines could be used when chairs evaluate their staff or when deans evaluate their chairs.

1. Conducting a Fair Appraisal

An evaluation interview is not productive if the session is based on an unfair or biased appraisal of faculty performance. A faculty member who believes the chair's evaluation is fair is less likely to react negatively to the appraisal's content. An important component of fairness is *consistency*. Faculty members who have performed similarly in teaching, research and service should earn like evaluations. The chair is asking for trouble if two faculty members with equal contributions receive unequal evaluations. And, the chair cannot be certain that faculty will not compare evaluations.

A fair appraisal takes into consideration variables outside of the faculty member's control that negatively affect his or her performance. At times faculty are assigned teaching overloads which hamper performance in teaching and research. Assignment to special departmental or institutional committees also takes a great deal of time. These and other demands should be taken into consideration.

To conduct a fair appraisal, the chair must be familiar with the faculty member's work. Chairs often require the faculty to prepare a summary of what has been accomplished over the past appraisal period. Summaries, however, do not substitute for firsthand knowledge of a faculty member's work. For instance, faculty should be observed in the classroom. Having the chair sit in on a class is often intimidating, unless the visits are considered a normal and supportive occurrence. The chair should let faculty members know the reason for the visit and set up a date for the visit (it does little good to sit in on an examination or a day of presentation by students). The chair should also read the course syllabi and materials each faculty member has *submitted* to conventions and journals, as well as those presented and published.

The *standards* used to evaluate faculty are also important. The evaluation process should not focus on irrelevant personality traits or subjective assessments. Rather, *the job performance of the faculty should be evaluated on objective standards*. In business, objective evaluation standards are generally easy to formulate. Employees may be appraised on the basis of how many products they make or how many sales they close. In academic institutions, the task of developing objective appraisal criteria is difficult, but not impossible. For faculty, student surveys of instruction provide quantitative data on which teaching ability may be evaluated. Journal publications, presentations to student groups and outside consulting projects may be counted. Certainly, not all faculty contributions may be reduced to numbers. However, to strive toward objectivity in the appraisal is desirable because subjective evaluations are inherently unfair, potentially biased and often result in discrimination, anger, grievances and law suits.

The chair should maintain an assessment file for each faculty member. (Some refer to this file as a "critical incidents" file, however, the term is pejorative with negatively perceived information.) Instead of trying to remember at the end of the year what the faculty did, when a chair hears a student complement or learns of a new faculty publication he or she should immediately make a note of it and place it in that person's assessment file. The assessment file should contain both positive and negative information. Examples of both good and bad behavior should be noted. At the end of the appraisal period, the file helps the chair document the faculty member's evaluation and better guarantees objectivity. Obviously, the chair should review the appraisal file prior to the appraisal interview.

2. Choosing an Appropriate Setting for the Interview

The setting for the appraisal interview often influences the discussion. Many chairs conduct appraisal interviews in their own offices. However, the best location for the interview lies in neutral territory. A neutral environment minimizes the chair's power and authority and insures a more productive and open discussion. A conference room is a good setting. If a conference room is unavailable, the interview should be conducted in a private office free from interruptions. The meeting location should be isolated from the normal flow of office traffic and telephone calls.

The environment should be as comfortable and non-threatening as possible. Skilled chairs have learned that faculty members engage in more self-disclosure when they sit side-by-side or at the adjoining corners of a table. If the chair and faculty member sit across from each other at a table or desk, physical and psychological barriers exist that hamper the discussion. Such an environment is more like a bargaining session than an appraisal interview and often produces competitive rather than cooperative behavior.

3. Properly Schedule the Interview

Appraisal interviews should be neither too long nor too short. The interview should not develop into a marathon session which tires both the chair and the faculty member. Very short interviews prevent the accomplishment of even modest appraisal goals. In addition, scheduling an interview of short duration may communicate that the appraisal process is not important. Proper scheduling also involves giving the faculty sufficient advance notice of when the interview is to occur. The chair should allow faculty enough time to prepare supporting materials and to document their activities relating to past accomplishments. This time can also be spent formulating future goals and objectives. Even if time is not needed for these tasks, the faculty requires time psychologically to gear up for the interview; so chairs should be sensitive to the faculty's need to mentally prepare for the event. Remember, faculty will put in as much, if not more, time preparing for the appraisal as will the chair.

4. Do Not Cover Past Performance and Expected Future Performance in the Same Interview

A good appraisal procedure actually consists of *two formal interviews* at the end of each appraisal cycle. The first interview is normally devoted to a discussion of the faculty member's work during the appraisal year. The faculty member's performance evaluation or rating evolves from the first interview. The second interview should take place a week or so after the first. This is a "development" conference, and it should center on the faculty member's goals and objectives for the upcoming academic year.

The rationale for a "split appraisal" scheme is simple. If the discussion resulting from the evaluation is combined with the development conference, the discussion of the evaluation dominates, and plans for development become overshadowed. Most faculty have difficulty concentrating on improving next year's productivity when they are worried about the chair's evaluation of last year's accomplishments. Only after the evaluation session is complete, and the faculty member has reflected on the ratings and evaluation, can attention turn to goal-setting.

5. Setting Appropriate Goals for Future Performance

The development phase of faculty evaluation is covered in detail in chapter 6. As noted in that chapter, faculty evaluation is a continual and renewing process in which the department and faculty continually re-examine and project their goals for the future. Keeping this in mind, the chair, in preparing for an appraisal interview, should remember several points. First, *clear and specific goals are superior to vague ones* like "do your best." For example, "improve research effort" is vague and general, whereas "submit two papers to national conventions" is clearer and more specific. A clear and specific goal sets a precise target at which the faculty member may aim. Compared to a nebulous goal, a clear and specific goal may generate more task motivation, interest, productivity and job satisfaction.

Second, *goals should be concrete, observable and measurable*. As noted earlier, fair evaluations result when review standards are fair. Concrete, observable and measurable goals are inherently objective. In the previous example, determining whether a faculty member's research efforts have improved is often difficult and subject to varied interpretations compared to determining whether two papers were submitted to national conventions.

Third, *the chair should give no more than two or three goals for the next appraisal period*. As the number of goals increases, the faculty member's time and energy expended also increases. Too many goals often result in no improvement in any area. It is the chair's responsibility to assess the faculty member's most pressing needs and then set goals accordingly. If, for example, the faculty member needs to improve in teaching and research, the chair should decide which area is most important and goals should be developed in that area first. If the faculty member is deficient in a number of skills related to teaching, goals should be formulated to correct the most critical problems immediately and the others later.

Fourth, *goals should be prioritized.* Even if only two or three goals are set, the faculty member should know which goal is considered most important. Knowing a goal's priority provides the faculty member an opportunity to budget his or her time.

Fifth, *goals should be adapted to the unique talents and interests of each faculty member.* Goals differ in their challenge. What challenges one faculty member may not challenge another. Obviously, different goals are needed for new versus tenured faculty. Goals typically increase in difficulty as the faculty member moves up in rank; the goal of making full professor usually has more difficult requirements — both in terms of qualitative and quantitative outcomes — than making associate professor. The chair needs to know faculty needs and aspirations and endeavor to create goals that are best suited for each.

These points should be considered as the chair prepares for the appraisal interview. Often it helps if the faculty member also considers them, preparing for his or her interview by reviewing past performance in achieving goals and what future goals might be.

6. Allow the Faculty Member to Participate in the Appraisal Process

When arriving at a performance evaluation, or when attempting to develop new goals for a faculty member, the chair has two choices. First, he or she may determine the evaluation or set new goals without input from the faculty.

Using this scheme, the chair discloses individual evaluations or new goals at the interview; the faculty are simply expected to accept the chair's sage advice and reasoning with little or no comment. The evaluation and goals are firmly fixed before the interview and, regardless of what is discussed during the interview, the evaluation and/or goals are not changed.

Second, the chair may request input from the faculty in the evaluation or goal-setting process. Whether the focus is evaluation or goal-setting, the interview is devoted to sharing ideas, negotiation and compromise. Rather than reaching a determination without the help of the faculty member, the chair develops an evaluation and a list of goals, all subject to modification. The faculty member is asked to conduct a self-evaluation on the assessment criteria established by the department or from previous appraisals and for a set of personal goals. This self-appraisal structures the first appraisal interview. The chair and faculty member then compare their evaluations and explore the reasons for any differences. When the session is complete, the chair decides on a final evaluation and communicates it to the faculty member. The faculty member's personal goals are the focus of the developmental interview. The chair and faculty member compare their goals and try to develop a composite set of goals satisfactory to both parties.

Appraisal interviews are more productive if the chair consults with faculty on both evaluations and new goals. Interviews in which the faculty participate are superior to chair-controlled interviews for several reasons. First, *most faculty dislike being treated in a dictatorial, authoritarian fashion.* Angry feelings and resentment often occur when the chair does not allow meaningful participation by the faculty in appraisal interviews. Second, *defensiveness and hostility on the part of the faculty is less when the faculty are allowed to help focus the discussions.* Criticism from others arouses more negative feelings than self-criticism and at times a faculty member's self-evaluation is harsher than the chair's evaluation. Third, *faculty goals are often more difficult and motivating than those envisioned by the chair.* People often expect more of themselves than do others and most people work harder to achieve a personal goal. Fourth, *participative interviews combine the resources and information of the faculty member and the chair.* Two-way communication and sharing of resources stimulate new insights and innovative solutions to problems.

Participative interviews are not appropriate for all faculty members. The style of the interview should be adapted to the individual. New faculty members, especially with little teaching experience, often lack the background required for self-appraisals and development of appropriate goals. Moreover, some faculty members prefer the chair to set the goals and control the interview. Generally, however, most faculty appreciate the opportunity to participate in the evaluation and goal-setting discussions. When in doubt, the chair should begin with maximum participation and then exercise greater control for those who need or request it.

7. Give Appropriate Praise and Criticism

In the evaluation interview, the chair must provide the faculty praise and criticism as needed. Unwarranted criticism may cause faculty members to be hostile and defensive. Surprisingly, unwarranted praise also has negative consequences. Faculty often question a chair's motives for giving praise and often feel manipulated when receiving it; alternatively, since praise implies an expectation for continued superior performance, it may threaten the faculty member, forcing him or her into a feeling of being trapped in a continuing spiral of superior performances.

Adverse reactions to praise and criticism are minimized if the chair remembers five things. First, *the amount of praise and criticism should be tailored to the faculty member being evaluated.* Faculty differ in their tolerance for praise and criticism. Some are disturbed by only modest amounts, while others may be praised or criticized to excess. The key is adapting the amount of praise or criticism to the faculty member's unique tolerance level.

Second, *praise and criticism should be given in an appropriate ratio.* In many appraisal interviews, a disproportionate amount of time is spent on criticism. If a faculty member is evaluated highly on eight of ten performance standards, eighty percent of the interview should be spent on praise.

Third, *the interview should begin with praise.* While praise may be given at any time in the appraisal interview, the first part of it should be devoted exclusively to praise. A faculty member is more receptive to criticism when the chair begins the interview by reviewing the faculty member's strengths.

This leads to the fourth point, *the chair should give objective praise and criticism.* Evaluations should always be based on objective, concrete, observable and measurable behaviors. Arguments are less likely if the chair can document a negative evaluation with statistics and/or specific examples from the faculty member's appraisal file. Likewise, the faculty member will feel less manipulated if the praise is sincere and based on real accomplishments.

Fifth, *praise and criticism should be oriented toward the future.* Although the appraisal interview is grounded in past performance, it should have a prospective dimension. Praise should not be given just for the sake of giving praise. Rather, it should reinforce good work habits and encourage continued performance in the future. The emphasis should not be on "you did well" but on "what can we do to insure your good performance continues?" Instead of just giving criticism, the chair should use it to explore ways to improve job performance. The focus should not be on the claim that "you did an unsatisfactory job;" the focus should be "how can this problem be avoided in the future?"

8. Establishing the Proper Communication Climate

The communication climate of the appraisal interview is very important. *Appraisal discussions are more productive if the chair approaches the interview with enthusiasm and a positive attitude.* Rather than verbally and nonverbally communicating "I don't look forward to these sessions but it's that time of the year again and we've got to go through this," the chair should effuse behaviors indicating that the appraisal interview is a valuable opportunity that can lead to improved relationships and professional growth. Even in interviews with faculty who are experiencing difficulties, the chair should be friendly, warm, supportive and genuinely interested in their problems. The chair must listen to what the faculty member says and express confidence in his or her ability to do the job. Chairs should not nag, preach, or talk down. Since most people naturally resist manipulation, appraisal interviews should be as spontaneous as possible and should not appear to have a hidden agenda.

The communication climate for the appraisal interview is more than the chair's behavior in the interview. The chair's daily behavior sets the tone for the interview. The chair cannot be hostile and controlling for 364 days and then be completely different on the day of the appraisal. Rather, the chair must continuously work to build a proper communication climate.

9. Do Not Limit Appraisal Discussions
to the Formal Appraisal Period

Appraisal is an ongoing process, not a once-a-year event. The chair should continually provide praise and criticism throughout the year, rather than waiting until the formal appraisal discussion to unload on the faculty member. As with appraisal, developmental conferences should also be conducted "informally" throughout the year. Often a milestone or an event (publication, grant, complement, as well as complaint) provides the impetus for an informal development discussion.

Some faculty may need more coaching than others. New faculty and faculty members with special problems may require weekly, monthly or quarterly informal review and planning sessions. A single formal session at the end of the year may be adequate for faculty who are performing up to expectations.

10. Summarize the Discussion

Every appraisal interview should end with a summary of the discussion. Most interviews involve many topics and issues that may be forgotten or lost if they are not itemized at the end of the interview. Before the interview ends, the chair and faculty member should review the agreements reached and the plans established for the next appraisal cycle. In most cases, the summary should be reduced to writing. A written summary of the interview often helps to prevent later uncertainties and misunderstandings. The formal document is then reviewed and signed by the faculty member and the chair.

Table 7.1
Chair's Pre-Appraisal Interview Checklist

1. Preparation

    _____ a. Review appraisal file
        _____ (1) Consistent with past performance
        _____ (2) Standards established at last review met
    _____ b. Review supporting documents
        _____ (1) Student surveys
        _____ (2) Classroom observations
        _____ (3) Syllabi and class handouts
        _____ (4) Convention papers submitted and/or accepted
        _____ (5) Manuscripts submitted and/or accepted for publication

2. Setting

    _____ a. Private
    _____ b. Comfortable
    _____ c. Nonthreatening

3. Scheduling

    _____ a. Advance notice
    _____ b. Length: _____ minutes

Table 7.1 continued

4. *Conference Type*

   _____ a. Performance Appraisal
   _____ b. Developmental

5. *Setting Goals*

   _____ a. Recommended number of goals: _____
   _____ b. Stated clearly and specifically
   _____ c. Outcomes measurable
   _____ d. Priority established
   _____ e. Adapted to
          _____ (1) Promotion
          _____ (2) Tenure
          _____ (3) Merit increase

6. *Faculty Participation*

   _____ a. Involved
          _____ (1) Self-evaluation
          _____ (2) Personal goals
          _____ (3) Chair's evaluation
          _____ (4) Chair's goals
   _____ b. Not involved
          _____ (3) Chair's evaluation
          _____ (4) Chair's goals

7. *Praise and Criticism*

   _____ a. Praise
          _____ (1) Teaching
          _____ (2) Research
          _____ (3) Service
   _____ b. Criticism
          _____ (1) Teaching
          _____ (2) Research
          _____ (3) Service
   _____ c. Strategy
          _____ (1) Percent praise: _____/Percent criticism: _____
          _____ (2) Praise categories: _____
          _____ (3) Criticism categories: _____
          _____ (4) Important categories: _____

Table 7.1 continued

8. *Climate*

    _____ a. Warm
    _____ b. Vital
    _____ c. Positive

9. *Planning for Next Cycle*

    _____ a. Formal reviews needed
        _____ (1) Frequency: _____
        _____ (2) Categories: _____
    _____ b. Informal reviews needed
        _____ (1) Frequency: _____
        _____ (2) Categories: _____
    _____ c. No intermediate reviews necessary

10. *Summary*

    _____ a. Points to emphasize
        _____ (1) Teaching
        _____ (2) Research
        _____ (3) Service
    _____ b. Written summary
        _____ (1) Agreements
        _____ (2) Signed
            _____ (a) No protest
            _____ (b) Under protest

Summary

The performance appraisal interview can be a traumatic event for some. However, if the chair approaches the task with the foregoing guidelines in mind, the appraisal interview should be more productive and enjoyable for both the chair and the faculty. Chairs need to remember that assessment and appraisal is a year-round process. Informal discussions with faculty often serve to verify adherence to plans and signify the faculty are on goal. It is important that the chair approach the evaluation process as a positive tool with which to engender faculty and departmental development.

CHAPTER 8

Being Assessed

Edward L. McGlone and
Susan K. Kovar

8:30   Met with dean for chair's appraisal.

12:30 Departmental brown bag re: chair's post- evaluation
leadership comments.

The average period of service for an academic department
chair is only about five years. This means that each year
about twenty thousand chairs at American post-secondary
institutions give up their positions. A few leave because they
are taking new administrative positions, some because they
want to "step down" and still others because of reassignment
due to faculty or dean dissatisfaction with their performance.

Why is there so much turnover among department chairs?
One might expect a lengthy tenure as chair to be the capstone
of a distinguished career. It is easy to understand why
successful chairs aspire to higher levels of administration.
But, why is there so much attrition? Because of frustration
or lack of success? It may be partially because most chairs
assume their position with little or no prior training or
experience. Additionally, the role of the chair is complex and
demanding, and the role has become even more demanding
in recent years. But part of the attrition explanation is simply

that we do not do a very good job of assessing how well chairs do their jobs.

A conscientious chair, like an untenured faculty member, needs to know how well he or she is doing. This presents a problem in communication management. Research tells us that asking for criticism is difficult for many people and that receiving criticism is even more trying. Most people find direct criticism threatening, and we have become accustomed to giving and getting criticism in indirect ways. A chair may see the assessment of faculty performance as a legitimate and essential task. He or she should not be surprised to learn that the chair's performance needs to be evaluated as well, although the two processes may differ.

There are legal and procedural requirements for evaluating faculty. As noted in other chapters, nearly every institution has a written description of the evaluation process for determining merit raises, promotions and tenure decisions. A chair must limit the evaluation to well-documented and "objective" statements. On the other hand, chairs typically serve at the "pleasure" of the dean. They often must survive elections in which the departmental faculty can vote "no confidence" without stating their reasons or even giving their names. There is nothing indirect about a vote of no confidence.

Also, as ambiguous as a faculty member's profession may be, there are specific teaching assignments and expectations for scholarship and service. *This is not always the case for a chair.* Some faculty expect their chair to function primarily as a facilitator and provider of resources. Others expect their chair to conduct meetings and advocate their causes to the dean and central administration who, in turn, require her or him to generate more FTE and to reduce spending. With all these expectations, chairs often see their most important role as providing departmental leadership by becoming the model for excellence in teaching, scholarship and service. But, as diverse as the expectations of a chair are, there is an equal diversity in the people who may judge his or her performance. The faculty, deans, vice presidents, president, other chairs, students, alumni, service unit administrators and departmental secretaries may have opinions about the quality of a chair's work. They also have their own ways of rewarding and penalizing his or her performance.

Our view is that *the chair, even a new chair, should take the initiative in clarifying the process by which he or she is assessed.* We believe that this should be done even if the institution has some general assessment procedure in place. Because chairs should receive accurate and reasonably complete information about their performance, periodic evaluations are better than a singular and possibly final "vote of confidence."

Who Should Assess the Chair's Performance?

The first question to be answered in clarifying the assessment process is, "Who should do the chair's assessment?" Unfortunately, a legitimate answer is, "Practically everybody." The chair of an academic department, like it or not, is a middle-management position. Chairs literally are in the middle and are accountable to a variety of constituencies, including the faculty, students, office staff, dean, central administration and other chairs. They are also accountable to themselves, and self-evaluation should be a part of any assessment process.

It is not always a matter of being able to determine which of these constituencies are the most important. New chairs sometimes think that their own faculty (or the faculty in their discipline generally) constitute their only important constituency. An effective chair, however, considers all these constituencies important.

Nevertheless, it is impractical to involve all constituencies in the assessment plan. The best compromise between an ideal procedure and a practical one is to seek evaluations from both superiors (the dean) and subordinates (the faculty) and to ask that these assessments include the evaluators' perceptions about the opinions of other constituents. Some chairs find it difficult to think of their faculty as subordinates, while others find it all too easy. It is unrealistic to view the chair as a peer of the faculty, when he or she influences faculty salaries, promotion and tenure, the assignment of office space and teaching assignments. It is equally unrealistic to expect to receive entirely candid evaluations from the faculty whose lives are influenced in these ways. The best advice is for the chair to do everything possible to insure the confidentiality of faculty evaluations — although some faculty resist anonymity — and then convince them that he or she really does seek their honest appraisals.

Deans may be more candid, although some dislike giving unhappy or bad news. Again, the chair should make it clear that he or she wants to know how to be a more effective chair, something the dean should be able to relate to.

Having asked for candid opinions, the chair must respond to them professionally. Most people are defensive about their capabilities. When a chair is ultimately accountable to a dean and to faculty members who do not understand how difficult the job can be, it may be hard for that chair to admit that he or she is less than a paragon of skill and competence. One should take the advice in good faith and good humor, and use it to become a better chair.

What Should Be Evaluated?

Chairs are typically evaluated in three areas. Two of these concern the chair's leadership abilities. The third deals with his or her communication — or, as in this case, administrative — style. *Academic leadership* is the first and most important criterion by which a chair's effectiveness is evaluated. Academic leadership includes the chair's efforts to foster good teaching and to stimulate scholarship in the department through the following: recruitment of faculty, curriculum development, setting and maintaining high standards in personnel decisions, implementing faculty development programs and working with the faculty as a mentor or a colleague.

The chair's credibility as an academic leader is affected by his or her performance as a faculty member. Performance is gauged by standing in the discipline and accomplishments in teaching, scholarship and professional service. *It is easier to lead by example than by prescription.* Having said this, a word of caution is in order. Some chairs exploit the position to enhance their *own* academic credentials. If the chair uses too large a share of the department's resources for their own professional activities, they are not providing good academic leadership.

A chair is also evaluated in terms of *administrative leadership.* Both the faculty and the dean are concerned about how the chair manages the business of the department: the fiscal matters, meeting of deadlines and other reporting requirements, and the dissemination of information. Also included in this category are some less mundane matters, such as the ability to delegate responsibilities and attention to governance guidelines and procedures. Some of the more abstract aspects of administrative leadership include the ability to seize opportunities when they are presented and the effect of the chair's activities on faculty morale.

Finally, a chair is evaluated on *communication management.* An effective chair is a good listener and a persuasive advocate. He or she is sensitive to human relationships and skillful in managing interpersonal communication. Effective chairs know how to conduct a meeting and how to be a constructive participant in one. They are able to flex their social style (Darling, 1985) along two dimensions of interpersonal communication behavior, assertiveness and responsiveness, in order to successfully exercise upward influence in the department.

Academic leadership, administrative leadership, and communication management are overlapping categories. Certainly a chair's ability to implement an "administrative" decision may be primarily affected by the credibility she or he has established as an academic leader and by his or her ability to communicate effectively. This close relationship among these three categories is helpful in understanding the valuations that may be made of a department chair's *administrative style.*

A new chair or a chair who is new to being assessed may question the legitimacy of judgments about his or her "style," because we would never countenance opinions about such matters in evaluations of faculty for merit raises, promotions, or tenure. Is it legitimate to evaluate how an administrator's personality and skills (i.e., administrative style) affect her or his abilities to motivate faculty, handle conflict, and make fair decisions?

The personal qualities or skills of the chair provide the "natural tendencies" used by that individual to perform a myriad of functions. These personal qualities include such things as courage, integrity, fairness, commitment, and respect for self and others. Personal qualities applied in professional situations become labelled as "administrative style" and as such they are appropriate subjects of evaluation. The personal qualities themselves are not subjected to evaluation, but the product that occurs when personal qualities are applied in professional situations is evaluated. For example, Tucker and Bryan (1988) discuss the performance problems (product) that chairs can have if they lack courage. They indicate that academic administrators who lack courage try to avoid controversy as much as possible and are often reluctant to take stands on various issues which can prove to be detrimental to programs and departments. We would agree with Tucker and Bryan and add the distinction that lack of the personal quality, "courage," leads to an administrative style that includes "fear of taking a stand" and the product of that style can be positive or negative depending on given circumstances. In general though, not taking a stand is viewed negatively as many deans criticize chairs for indecisiveness.

Therefore, just as student evaluations of teaching performance will vary according to the size, level, and other aspects of the nature of the course being taught, so should evaluations of a chair be affected by the nature of the department. The effectiveness of the administrative style reflected in the chair's academic leadership, administrative leadership, and communication management depends on the nature of the department. A very effective chair of a small department which offers an undergraduate curriculum may not do well at all in a similar post in a large doctoral-degree granting program. The reverse of this situation is also true. It is important for the evaluation criteria to "fit" the context of the evaluation. If evaluation criteria are specific to the department, then the desired product (administrative performance) is known. Given a desired product, the chair can be evaluated in terms of how well their administrative style serves to produce effective academic leadership, administrative leadership, and communication management.

A chair's administrative style is difficult, if not impossible, to change because its roots are firmly planted in the personal qualities of the individual. A chair who has a "natural tendency" not to share information will probably not share information often with faculty. This non-sharing of information can be viewed either positively or negatively, depending on the department. If viewed negatively, the chair might be able to change his or her behavior. If the total administrative style of a chair does not fit the department, most chairs cannot adapt their styles; therefore, they seek other positions more suited to their style of administration.

Should the Assessment Be Formal or Informal?

Communication research tells us that direct personal contact is almost always more effective than an exchange of written messages. Similarly, the most effective evaluations are informal and face-to-face. Formal written evaluations become a part of the chair's permanent record; and they may be required for legal or procedural reasons. It is good for the chair to remember, however, that formal evaluations can be made more meaningful if they are accompanied or supplemented by frequent personal interaction.

A chair should seek both an assessment interview with the dean and collect input from the faculty. Faculty input can come informally, through conversations with the chair, or from formal evaluation instruments. In any event, the assessment interview usually follows a formal written evaluation of the chair. The formal interview should not be used by the chair as an opportunity for self-defense. Instead, the emphasis should be on understanding why the evaluation came out as it did, why certain perceptions have developed. The faculty and the chair, and the dean and the chair, must agree that their best interests are dependent on the success of the chair.

Evaluation Instruments

That said, we now turn to possible instruments for formal chair evaluations. Just as the evaluation criteria vary according to the nature of the department, so is the format of the chair's evaluation instrument affected by the people doing the evaluation. Some would say that mathematicians and scientists like to use numerical ratings, while humanists and artists prefer open-ended questionnaires. That has not been our experience, but it is true that different deans and different groups of faculty have different views on the matter. The ambiguity of the chair's position encourages the use of an open-ended format; but administrative requirements usually favor the use of more objective rating scales. At the very least, any rating scale should be accompanied by written comments explaining or elaborating on the ratings assigned.

There are a number of approaches for conducting formal evaluations of a chair's performance. The most comprehensive scheme we know about was developed at Kansas State University by its Center for Faculty Evaluation and Development.[1]

Figures 8.1 and 8.2 present two evaluation instruments that have been used in formal assessments of departments chairs. The first is a highly structured rating scale, intended for use by the departmental faculty. The second represents the other extreme, an open-ended questionnaire that could be used by either the faculty or the dean. Both instruments are based on forms developed by faculty committees and used at Emporia State University. A third instrument (see Figure 8.3) is included in a description of a comprehensive plan for involving the faculty and dean in the assessment of chairs within a particular school or college. The questionnaire combines numerical ratings and the opportunity for explanatory comments. The plan is based on a procedure developed by a committee on which one of the authors served at Southern Illinois University at Carbondale.

Figure 8.1
Structured Rating Scale for
Assessing the Chair's Performance (ESU)

Chair's Evaluation

Name of Chair _____ Date _____
Department _____

In order to help The Teachers College appraise the effectiveness of its administrative personnel, you are requested to evaluate your division chair in five dimensions. The highest rating is 5 and the lowest is 1. Please circle the numeral that represents your considered opinion of your chair. Three of the five possible ratings are described by phrases printed to the left of the numerals. You may also use intermediate numerals for the expression of your opinions.

ADMINISTRATIVE DIMENSION	DESCRIPTIVE PHRASES	RATING
Is he or she accessible and approachable in personal or non-professional matters?	Has good rapport with faculty members; always ready and willing to discuss personal problems; takes a genuine interest and is usually helpful.	5 4
	Available to discuss problems; takes interest and makes some effort to be helpful; easy to approach	3
	Too busy to talk; does not seem to want to be involved; makes only routine responses; takes only perfunctory interest.	2 1
Is s/he accessible and approachable in professional or academic matters?	Always ready and willing to discuss professional problems; takes a genuine interest in each faculty member's professional growth; always tries to be helpful and usually is helpful; approaches problems and suggestions with an open mind.	5 4
	Available to discuss problems; gives consideration to problems and suggestions; hesitates to make changes; generally tries to keep an open mind.	3 2

Figure 8.1 continued

Too busy to talk; concerned only about his own problems and interests; shows only perfunctory interest in proposals and suggestions of staff members.　　　1

ADMINISTRATIVE DIMENSION	DESCRIPTIVE PHRASES	RATING
Are decisions regarding utilization of departmental personnel made with appropriate consideration of faculty abilities and interests?	Discusses teaching assignments with faculty before schedules are made; demonstrates flexibility in reviewing assignments and schedules; gives consideration to academic rank and seniority but has more concern about individual abilities and interests; does not "play favorites"; provides for orientation of faculty new to the department; effective in evaluation of staff.	5 4
	Develops schedules and makes assignments without prior discussions with individual faculty members; resists reviewing assignments; considers rank and seniority as important as individual abilities and interests; most evaluations are valid.	3 2
	Makes arbitrary decisions and assignments without explanations and discussions; does not review or change assignments; "plays favorites"; lacks objectivity in evaluations of staff.	1
Are departmental affairs well managed?	Has good organizational ability; gets routine matters cared for with dispatch; major policies, issues and problems are discussed at department meetings; develops adequate procedures to implement policies; distributes departmental equipment, materials and supplies fairly; budgets are forward-looking and realistic; promotes good relationships among faculty in the department; fosters the development of morale.	5 4

Figure 8.1 continued

Frequently takes too much time for
routine matters; major policies and pro-   3
blems are discussed but some decisions
are not implemented; shows some concern about relations among faculty and
department morale; budgets show some
planning.   2

Department equipment and supplies are
not fairly distributed; budgets are poorly
planned and unrealistic; department
meetings are given over to routine and
perfunctory matters; offers little or no
leadership in human relationships.   1

ADMINISTRATIVE DIMENSION	DESCRIPTIVE PHRASES	RATING
Are departmental academic programs and needs properly coordinated and emphasized?	Has adequate academic and subject matter competence; effective in recruiting staff; involves appropriate staff members in recruiting decisions; has good relations with other administrators; acquires adequate departmental resources; causes departmental programs and activities to be evaluated and reviewed; provides effective leadership or support to the development of well-balanced and forward-looking departmental programs; presses for intra-departmental and inter-departmental communication regarding subject content.	5 4
	Has average academic competence; occasionally involves other staff members in recruitment; has satisfactory relations with other administrators; makes some effort to acquire departmental programs; usually encourages communication between and within departments.	3 2
	Inadequate academic and subject matter background; ineffective in recruitment of staff members; does not work easily or effectively with other administrators; desires adequate departmental resources	1

Figure 8.1 continued

but does not make proper effort to
acquire the same; interest in the courses
he teaches but takes little interest in
developing departmental programs; dis-
courages communication between and
within departments.

Additional Comments:

Figure 8.2
Open-Ended Questionnaire for
Assessing the Chair's Performance (ESU)
Chair's Evaluation

Department of _____

1. What do you consider to be the Chair's significant strengths?

2. What do you consider the Chair's most significant weaknesses?

3. Overall, how would you assess the Chair's performance during the past
year? (please circle)

Very High   5   4   3   2   1   Very Low

Additional Comments:

Figure 8.3
Procedure for Assessing
the Chair's Performance (SIU-C)

Administrative Evaluation

Purpose:
Administrative evaluation is vital to the organization and operation of the College. It is designed to promote the creative, technical, conceptual, and human skills associated with a position and with the individual occupying the position. The evaluation is to allow for a free and candid exchange among all those involved in the process.

Procedures:
To implement the reviews of the chairs and directors, the Dean will meet with the total faculty of the department/school. The unit executive officer will not attend this meeting. The Dean will discuss procedures and the evaluation instrument. Each faculty member will be given a copy of the instrument and will be asked to return it to the Dean in a sealed envelope by a specified date. All envelopes will be opened personally by the Dean, who will make a composite summary of responses for each chair/director. After the established procedures are completed, the Dean will destroy the original signed copies. The summary will be discussed with the chair or director and a copy will be placed in the chair's/director's personnel file. Next will be a meeting with the unit's faculty (again in the absence of the chair/director), at which time the Dean will report the outcome of the evaluation. After this meeting, the Dean will discuss this outcome with the chair or director.

The Evaluation Form:
A basic objective of evaluation is to identify both strengths and weaknesses in performance. Comments are welcomed on any or all response items. The evaluator is urged to provide factual action-oriented statements rather than broad generalizations.

Dept./School _____ Chair/Dir. _____

I. PERFORMANCE CRITERIA FOR EVALUATING DIRECTORS OR CHAIRPERSONS

Please evaluate the director of your school or the chairperson of your department on the following "Performance Criteria." *For each criterion indicate your rating of the individual on a scale of "1" to "5," with "1" being the lowest rating and "5" the highest.* Leave blank those items you have not had the opportunity to observe and evaluate.

Figure 8.3 continued

A. ACADEMIC LEADERSHIP

_____ 1. Articulates academic goals for the department or school, and demonstrates innovation, skill, and persistence in attaining them.

Comments:_____

_____

_____ 2. Demonstrates a thorough understanding of the nature and variety of academic programs found in the discipline(s) represented in the department or school.

Comments:_____

_____

_____ 3. Evidences personal involvement in continuing scholarship, through activity in research, creative work, writing, reading, and publishing.

Comments:_____

_____

_____ 4. Understands contemporary problems and issues in his/her discipline.

Comments:_____

_____

_____ 5. Is firmly committed to academic freedom and the principle of due process, and articulates ways and means to protect and attain each.

Comments:_____

_____

_____ 6. Recognizes and nurtures creative scholarship in the department or school.

Comments:_____

_____

Figure 8.3 continued

B. CONSTITUENCY LEADERSHIP

_____ 1. Recognizes and effectively deals with the organizational and functional elements of the institutional structure of the university, as related to both inter- and intra-departmental and school interests.

Comments:_____

_____

_____ 2. Involves all academic personnel in governance procedures of the department or school.

Comments:_____

_____

_____ 3. Delegates appropriate authority and responsibility to faculty and staff.

Comments:_____

_____

_____ 4. Is responsive to the academic needs of the faculty and students of the department or school.

Comments:_____

_____

_____ 5. Is fair to all constituents in decision-making.

Comments:_____

_____

_____ 6. Builds and keeps high morale in the department or school.

Comments:_____

_____

C. EXECUTIVE SKILLS

_____ 1. Possesses managerial skills and a managerial style that insures effective leadership of departmental or school constituency.

Comments:_____

_____

Figure 8.3 continued

_____ 2. Identifies the central issues of personnel and managerial problems in the department or school, and structures and articulates practical solutions to those problems.

Comments:_____

_____

_____ 3. Demonstrates leadership in state-of-the-art curriculum and program changes.

Comments:_____

_____

_____ 4. Expertly manages fiscal matters.

Comments:_____

_____

D. PERSONAL CHARACTERISTICS

_____ 1. Demonstrates sensitivity to human relationships among individuals in the constituency.

Comments:_____

_____

_____ 2. Listens to and responds to constituent viewpoints, and incorporates them wherever and whenever possible in decisions for, and operations of, the department or school.

Comments:_____

_____

_____ 3. Manifests the following characteristics, to insure confidence and support from his/her departmental or school constituency:

_____ a. Integrity

Comments:_____

_____

Figure 8.3 continued

_____ b. Humaneness

Comments:_____

_____

_____ c. Patience

Comments:_____

_____

_____ d. Fairness

Comments:_____

_____

II. Please indicate what, in your opinion, are the *positive qualities* of your chairperson or director, relative to his/her academic and administrative leadership of your department or school.

III. Please indicate what are, in your opinion, the *negative qualities* of your department chairperson or director, relative to his/her academic and administrative leadership of your department or school.

VOTE OF CONFIDENCE ON DEPARTMENT CHAIRPERSON OR SCHOOL DIRECTOR

_____ I recommend that the chairperson or director of my department or school be continued in this position.

_____ I recommend that the chairperson or director of my department or school *not* be continued in this position.

_____
Signature

_____
Date

How Often Should Assessments Occur?

A periodic assessment helps a chair to see his or her progress or lack of progress over time. This is especially helpful after a chair has undergone a series of evaluations. But it is extremely important that the chair seek assessment during periods of institutional change. This is even more true when the chair has been *mandated* as the agent of change. Such periodic evaluation becomes essential in determining whether goals have been met and when not met in gaining an understanding of why they were not attained.

Many institutions now mandate periodical "leadership reviews" of chairs and deans. If such a procedure is not implemented at the chair's institution, our advice is to seek formal assessments annually from the dean and every three to five years from the faculty. This is consistent with the practice at institutions where chair assessments have been implemented on an institution-wide basis. It also makes sense in terms of the chair's goals in seeking a formal assessment.

Using the Assessment

How the chair responds to an appraisal is possibly the most difficult communication problem to manage in the entire assessment process. The chair who becomes defensive or hostile in response to criticism learns little from the evaluation. We suggest the following five principles be used as a guide when a chair interprets the results of an assessment.

1. *Preview the results of the evaluation from the chair's own self-assessment.* A good chair often sets higher standards for his or her own performance than either faculty or dean. So, the chair should find out how his or her personal assessment compares with that of the faculty. It is also helpful for the chair to personally complete the evaluation form as he or she expects the faculty and dean to do. More often than not, the chair knows what complaints and compliments will be received. The exercise often leads to self-growth as the chair compares his or her self-evaluation to others.

2. *Do not make a personal judgment about the motives behind unfavorable criticism.* The chair should try to remember how he or she viewed their chairs before becoming one. Most faculty do not realize that a chair's feelings can be hurt by severe criticism. It is possible that some faculty might want to make the chair look bad, but chairs cannot afford to allow this possibility to interfere with their ability to learn from the evaluation process. Our advice is to review the evaluations with a senior chair, especially one who has had more experience with the assessment process. A chair may discover that a criticism thought to be motivated by jealousy or envy is a fairly common complaint. In any case, experienced chairs can better comment on the evaluations' fairness and objectivity.

3. *Do not contradict a request for an honest appraisal with negative reactions.* The simple fact is that the evaluation process invites the faculty and the dean to "lay it on the line." If the chair becomes defensive, he or she convinces them that the request for honesty was not sincere. This can affect the way both the dean and the faculty see subsequent requests from the chair. One of the personal qualities a chair must strive toward is the ability to take criticism and learn from it.

4. *Do follow up on the assessment.* In an interview with the dean or at a faculty meeting, a chair should summarize what was learned from the evaluations and what the plans are for acting on the information. When the dean and the faculty know that the chair is paying attention to their suggestions, they respond more enthusiastically to subsequent requests for their participation and they respect the chair more.

5. *Do indicate appreciation to those who gave honest evaluations.* This is simply another way of reinforcing the behavior sought. It also relieves any tension that may have been created by the evaluation process and helps to build a climate of trust and cooperation.

The chair's reaction to an assessment often tells a lot about his or her communication style. Chairs who approach the evaluation process with a positive outlook, who are seeking information about their performance as a way of helping the department achieve its goals, often find the dean and the faculty supportive. It is important that assessments pave the way for improved performance. Just as the chair's assessment of his or her faculty helps them meet their goals and challenges them toward still higher goals, the faculty and dean's assessment of the chair should strive for similar administrative and leadership outcomes.

Summary

Periodic assessments should not replace spontaneous and instantaneous feedback. The chair, sometimes with little help from potential evaluations, should work to establish a permissive environment in which the faculty are encouraged to communicate their criticism and suggestions without waiting for a formal evaluation. The particular mix of chair and dean often determines whether immediate feedback is likely in that relationship.

Fostering an atmosphere of trust encourages permissiveness on the part of both the faculty and the dean. The best way to win trust is to be trusting of others. That may seem overly simplistic, but successful administrators and managers in and out of academia agree on the advice. A chair who demonstrates that he or she trusts the faculty and the dean to be fair and honest in their evaluations reinforces his or her credibility as a leader. It also helps to foster a work climate of mutual trust and a focus on common goals.

References

Darling, J. R. (1985). Managing up in academe: The role of social style. *Texas Tech Journal of Education, 12*, 79–82.

Tucker A., and Bryan, R. A. (1988). *The academic dean: Dove, dragon, and diplomat.* New York: ACE/Macmillan.

1. DECAD (Departmental Evaluation of Chairperson Activities for Development) is a comprehensive system for assessing department chairs. For information, write to the Center for Faculty Evaluation and Development, Division of Continuing Education, Kansas State University, Manhattan, Kansas 66506.

CHAPTER 9

Departmental Assessment

Patti Peete Gillespie

11:00 Met with chairs for program on departmental assessment.

4:00 Met with dean to discuss plans for departmental assessment.

Academic institutions are increasingly engaged in self-study. They are assessing their mission and, more importantly, their colleges', divisions', and departments' contributions to that mission. This chapter explores departmental assessment and the chair's role in its mechanics.

Although few people question the importance of assessment, there is disagreement over its nature and function. Should assessment rest on human judgment or objective instruments? Should criteria be based on minimal standards or ideal expectations? Should a program's success be judged by its campus offerings or by the success of its graduates or by the "value added" during college (a value obtained by comparing the knowedge of entering and exiting students)? Because there is no consensus about what assessment should do, any discussion of it must acknowledge competing claims and must allow for institutional differences.

143

Assessment: What Is It?

For most purposes, *assessment, appraisal,* and *evaluation* mean *to set a value on* or *estimate the worth of.* Departmental assessments (like faculty or chair appraisals) aim simply to discover the strengths and weaknesses of a program of study. *Accreditation* includes, as an additional step, *certification.* Accreditation is of two sorts, institutional and programmatic. In institutional accreditation, an organization like the Southern Association of Colleges and Schools, after sending a team including representatives of many different disciplines and administrative levels to campus, certifies that the institution meets the standards of the Association. Such certification guides other agencies in deciding whether to accept transfer students, approve loads, or offer financial assistance. In programmatic assessment, an organization like the National Association of Music, after sending a team of music specialists to the campus to study its music program, certifies the institution's music discipline is healthy. Certification alerts prospective students and faculty in music that the program has met that field's national standards.

Assessment precedes all accreditation, but not all assessment results in (or is meant to result in) accreditation. Although departments participate in institutional assessment, its focus is on the institution not the department. In contrast, programmatic assessment focuses on the department and is the responsibility of the department.

Programmatic Assessment:
Who, When, and For What Purpose?

Healthy departments continuously evaluate their programs to identify achievements and deficiencies. More and more departments are now undertaking a regular, formal assessment as well. This formal assessment, typically conducted about every five years, involves some combination of departmental self-study and extra-departmental review.

Departmental faculty may undertake the self-study alone or with faculty from other departments on campus. A self-study committee may formulate its own questions and criteria, or it may use a standardized format provided by the institution or a professional association. Outside experts, who come to campus before, during, but most often after the self-study, may be asked to evaluate the department or simply to validate its self-study. Their views may be included in the report of an on-campus review committee. Because experts from off campus are so often used, many professional associations now maintain a list of approved consultants.

Among the several possibilities, the most common arrangement is to have departmental faculty conduct a self-study. The self-study, along with other materials, is mailed to two or three outside reviewers. After reviewing the self-study, these external reviewers visit the campus to answer questions they have regarding the department's conclusions and recommendations. The campus visit modifies impressions, answers lingering questions, and sometimes uncovers additional strengths and weaknesses.

A good assessment serves not only the needs of the department but also the institution's administration and the discipline nationally. The department, its own assessment verified or modified, is in a strong position to build on strengths and ameliorate weaknesses. The administration, having learned about national expectations of the field and about the relative position of its department within those expectations, can make more informed judgments about the department's position within the institution in terms of such matters as space, personnel, and operating funds. The discipline benefits each time a department within it is strengthened.

The best assessments occur when all parties undertake the assessment seriously and honestly. Departments who use assessment to self-promote rather than self-study, administrators who use appraisals as hatchets for cutting departments, and outside evaluators who strive to please rather to assess all subvert the process.

Assessment: What Factors Matter?

Across institutions and accrediting bodies, there is remarkable agreement about which factors ought to be considered in a departmental evaluation. The major issues are organization and governance, faculty, curriculum, students and graduates, facilities and equipment, and support. A miscellaneous category captures remaining concerns. The substance of each category can be made clear by suggesting the kinds of questions likely to be posed within it.

Organization and Governance

Organization refers both to the department's position within the institution and to its own internal structure. Information about the former is usually available in the college catalogue or in the campus's plan of organization. Information about the latter comes from interviews and from the department's materials, including procedures, by-laws and faculty minutes.

To provide a context for the remainder of the assessment, reviewers will want to begin with questions such as these:

> Is the department grouped with similar units (e.g., are all the arts in a separate college)?
>
> If not, is it grouped with compatible units (e.g., are the arts with speech and radio-television-film or with language and literatures)?
>
> Is the department's size comparable with others in the school or unit?
>
> If not, should the department be divided into parts or consolidated with other campus units?
>
> Are all reporting lines clear and sensible?
>
> Does the department have clear goals?
>
> Do these goals contribute to the goals of the institution?

Department governance is inevitably tied to institutional governance. Although a department can change only itself, it must understand itself in terms of the institution. Reviews can often help clarify matters of governance by posing questions like these:

How are decisions made above the department?

What structures exist so that the department can influence these decisions?

Are departmental faculty represented in appropriate governance bodies on campus?

Are departmental policies easily accessible and well understood?

Are there regular faculty meetings?

Are minutes published in a timely fashion?

Does the work of the department get done by the appropriate people, in appropriate ways, and within appropriate time limits?

Do students have an opportunity to be heard on matters affecting them?

Is the chair providing leadership and managing departmental resources effectively?

Are senior administrators and departmental faculty satisfied with the chair's leadership?

Faculty

Because the quality of its faculty is central to excellence within any department, special care should be taken in this part of the self-study. Faculty vitae can help to answer important questions like the following:

Do faculty have terminal degrees — from institutions recognized as excellent within the discipline?

Is there a good mix among the institutions represented by the faculty? (Several faculty hired from a single institution, or worse, from the institution where they now teach may signal an unhealthy situation.)

Is the faculty well distributed among the various ranks?

Is there evidence that the faculty remains intellectually vital? (Are they publishing? Are they active in professional and/or scholarly associations?)

148   *Patti Peete Gillespie*

Are the faculty who supervise graduate students qualified to do so by virtue of their record of publication or artistic professional work?

Do the faculty compare favorably with faculty at similar institutions?

Because good faculty, like good students, are learning as well as teaching, departments need to encourage faculty growth. To do so, a department must evaluate faculty and help faculty to act on the results of such evaluations. These requirements suggest another set of useful questions:

Does the department have written and readily accessible procedures for evaluating faculty?

Are the procedures for evaluating teaching, research or creative activity, and service sufficiently detailed to guide tenure, reappointment, or promotion reviews?

Do all faculty understand these procedures and perceive them as fair?

How often do evaluations take place, and who participates in them?

Are the department's teaching loads in line with the institution's expectations for research?

Does the department or institution offer resources for improving teaching and research? (Workshops? Travel funds? Course reductions? Semester's leave? Sabbatical grants?)

Is special attention given to shaping young faculty in their teaching and research?

Are intellectually (or artistically) vigorous faculty rewarded commensurate with their contributions to the department and discipline?

Do the salaries of faculty reflect their achievements?

Are salaries comparable to salaries at similar institutions?

Curriculum

Next to the faculty, the curriculum is probably the most important area of review; therefore, a careful study of the college catalogue, the syllabi of courses, several representative tests, and (in the case of graduate programs) samples of comprehensive examinations, theses, and dissertations are important. Some reasonable relationship between the faculty and the curriculum should be clear:

> Are there enough faculty to offer the advertised courses regularly?
>
> Are the areas of faculty interest and competence matched by the curriculum?
>
> Are there enough faculty to serve the number of students in each specialization?

Faculty cannot be expected to do everything equally well. Choices must be made about course and specialties to offer. Because departmental offerings do not exist independent of the institution, some questions about the context of the curriculum are important:

> Is the department making good use of courses in other disciplines within the university? (If one department offers courses in graduate statistics, must other departments in the same college or division offer their own?)
>
> Is the department making good use of curricular opportunities afforded by its location? (A department of biology in Maine that did not offer work in forestry would seem to be missing an opportunity.)
>
> Is the department making good use of educational activities outside of traditional classrooms? (Is the production program in theatre well-integrated with its instructional program? Are internships and cooperative education available, carefully and well-integrated with the curriculum?)

Finally, the department must display coherence: curricula must fit with faculty, courses with courses. To assure coherence, the review should begin with such questions as these:

Is the advertised curriculum actually offered?

Are the requirements for the major, the minor, and each specialization reasonable?

Do all such requirements resemble practices in comparable programs?

Is the departmental curriculum balanced appropriately with major/non-major courses; liberal arts/professional emphases; graduate/undergraduate work; various specializations?

Is there a reasonable balance between breadth and depth within each curriculum?

Are there any specializations or degrees that need to be eliminated or combined with other related curricula either within the department or the college?

Can a need for each specialization and each degree be demonstrated?

Students and Graduates

A department's students and graduates should be compared with those of comparable institutions and with those of other departments in the institution. Comparing standardized test scores, grade point averages, and writing samples is often helpful, as is comparing the ratios of students applying to those admitted, of those admitted to those attending, and of those entering to those graduating. Comparing available student aid for undergraduates and stipends for graduate students with those at comparable institutions is also important. All such data aim to help in answering questions like these:

Why are students attracted to the department and its programs?

How do they learn of the program?

Are the admitted students well qualified?

Do they receive appropriate advice and counseling?

Do they graduate after a reasonable time? Are they successful upon graduation?

Student opinions are helpful in assessing the quality of classroom teaching, the commitment of faculty to careful advising, the availability of faculty outside of class, the department's efforts to place its graduates, and the educational climate of the department. Students can help answer two important questions:

Does the department practice truth in advertising?

Does the department take its role as a teaching unit seriously?

In the case of graduate departments, the role of graduate students in undergraduate education needs to be carefully explored:

Are graduate teaching assistants carefully selected for their competence to undertake their assignments?

Are they well-trained for their tasks by the department?

Are they closely supervised?

Do they understand their dual role as teacher and as student? Are they clear about which takes priority? (Is the faculty clear about this as well?)

Student *perceptions* about the quality of their education can be secured by questionnaire or interview or both. The opinions of both current and matriculated students should be gathered, analyzed, and assessed.

Facilities and Equipment

Some research and instructional programs are more heavily dependent on facilities and equipment than others: research into small-group interaction requires more equipment than research into sixteenth-century French poetry; instruction in dance requires more space than instruction in medieval history. The core question for any review is simple: "Are facilities and equipment appropriate for the instructional and research mission of the department?"

Because faculty seldom think they have enough space or equipment, the review must rely on data in addition to faculty perception. Comparative information is available for many fields through professional associations, and some states have standards for allocating space and equipment: some number of square feet is required for each faculty member, each graduate student, each undergraduate major, each credit hour generated; some number of pianos is required for each piano faculty member and piano student. In some disciplines (chemistry, art studio), minimum standards may define the number and characteristics of specialized spaces and equipment. To these objective data, reviewers must add their own experiences as they attempt to evaluate the faculty's perception of need.

Square footage alone is seldom an adequate measure of facilities, and simple quantity of equipment is often irrelevant. A careful review should explore questions like these:

Is the available space well-used?

Is an appropriate range of spaces available: offices, lecture halls, seminar rooms, laboratories, etc.?

Are the spaces where they need to be?

Are there spaces to encourage interaction among faculty and students?

Are spaces well maintained?

Is money available for minor modifications to improve existing spaces where appropriate?

Is sufficient equipment available for both the curricular offerings and the faculty's research?

Is the equipment up-to-date?

Is there an appropriate range of equipment (e.g., sturdy and simple sound systems for beginning undergraduate instruction; sophisticated, state-of-the-art systems for research)?

Is all equipment working and well-maintained?

Is there a schedule for its maintenance and replacement?

Support

Instruction and research require some combination of clerical staff, professional staff, computers, studios, laboratories, audio-visual materials, libraries, etc. Although few departments have enough of everything they want, some departments are crippled by their deficiencies. If faculty must spend time in a history department doing clerical chores or in a theatre department building sets and costumes, that department is undersupported. If studios are not available for painters, or carrels for doctoral students, then the institution is not providing enough support. Because computer technology is changing so rapidly, a review should consider not only what computer-related items are now available, but also what plans exist for upgrading. Again, some professional associations and some institutions have guidelines that may aid in a review. Such guidelines are generally expressed as, for example, the number of clerical staff needed per faculty member. If such guidelines are available, a comparison of the department's status with that of other units in the institution and with those in comparable institutions help the committee reach sound conclusions. An effective chair will know of such guidelines and will provide them to the self-study committee.

Miscellaneous

Institutions may have specific questions they want answered. Such questions are usually based on the mission and history of the program under review. Many institutions now, for example, wish an outsider's assessment of their progress toward educational diversity, specifically their success at increasing the representation of women and minorities in the educational process. Questions that may help get at these issues include the following:

What is the percentage of non-white, non-male faculty at each rank and in each administrative position?

How does this percentage compare with the percentages of female and minority students?

Are there evident salary differences among races or genders? If so, are these explicable in terms of achievement and experience?

Are the catalogues, syllabi, examinations, and so forth, free of sexist language? (*Man and His World* may not be the best title for a course; references to professors and students only as *he* may be equally unwise.)

Are there required or recommended courses in which the contributions of women, ethnic Americans, and non-Western cultures receive prominent attention?

Are issues of race, gender, class, etc., raised appropriately in classes?

Do either female or minority faculty or students complain of discomfort or harassment in the department?

Assessment: Off-Campus Expert

Although institutions differ in the way they choose off-campus evaluators, most contact the professional association for a list of approved program evaluators. If no list exists, then the chair may be asked to identify nationally respected experts who can be called in to review the department and its self-study. A chair should welcome an objective, dispassionate review.

As representative of a discipline, off-campus evaluators have special responsibilities. Both the department and university's administration expect them to be knowledgeable of national practices, sensitive to institutional differences, and immune from the history and politics of the department under review. Their role is not to tell a department what to do, but rather to offer ideas about how a department might better do what it wants to do. If the goals of a department are unclear or are distant from nationally-accepted practices, the outside experts raise questions aimed at focusing the department's attention to its mission. Outside reviewers do not direct a department; rather they help a department see its divergence from nationally-accepted expectations and practices.

Outside experts have the advantage of being outside the day-to-day workings of the department. Faculty and students may confide in them and trust them to carry unpleasant messages to administrators. To encourage internal discussions of a problem or to act directly on the problem (with authorization from the administration) is an important part of an outside reviewer's responsibility.

Because site visits last usually one or two days, department chairs should help outside reviewers arrive well-prepared by sending all relevant materials as early as possible. External reviewers should arrive with a list of additional questions they want to explore and a list of additional materials they want to see during the visit. The chair should assure that an agenda of these reviewers provides opportunities to study the new materials, tour the relevant facilities, and meet with the people they need to interview.

A typical agenda for external reviewers begins with their meeting campus administrators, who usually provide an institutional context for the department under study, suggest specific questions to which the administration seeks answers, and describe the limitations under which the department works. Administrators usually make clear that few, if any, additional funds are available and urge reviewers to spend their time thinking of better ways to utilize existing funds. At or near the end of the site visit, the reviewers usually meet again with administrators, giving them the substance of their evaluation, previewing the final report, and settling on a timetable for the final report.

Early on the agenda, too, is a meeting with the departmental chair. He or she also provides context, suggesting additional questions for study, and describes the support given the department, accounting, if possible, for the level of that support. If the department has a self-study committee, the reviewers meet with it early in the visit. Then come tours of facilities, visits to classes, group and individual interviews, and study sessions. Most site visits provide an exit interview between the departmental faculty and the reviewers where a discussion of the process, a summary of major findings, and a preview of the final report invite correction of errors before the reviewers leave campus.

Assessment: The Mechanics

Assessment proceeds in five steps: deciding on the procedures for the assessment; deciding what information to gather; gathering the information; assessing the information; writing the final report.

Deciding on The Procedures for the Assessment

The department most often works with the administration to establish the general procedures of the assessment. If accreditation is to follow, the professional association may help with these early plans. Among the matters requiring decisions are the size and composition of the internal committee(s), the number and selection of off-campus reviewers, the administrative support for the review, and the timetable. Once these decisions are made, the department typically contacts committee members and outside evaluators, establishes meeting times, mails all materials, and facilitates the whole process.

Deciding What Information to Gather

The department (both chair and faculty), the administration, professional association, and outside reviewers may all take part in deciding what information to gather. In institutions where periodic assessment is required, the administration may request standard information of all departments; in fields where accreditation is to follow, professional associations may require answers to specific questions. In light of their own experiences, departmental faculty will wish to confirm impressions of weaknesses and strengths and so will generate questions. Outside reviewers may ask for additional information once they receive the self-study. In general, questions of the sort suggested in the preceding section will be asked, along with others based on the particular situation.

Gathering the Information

Major responsibility for gathering the data rests with the department. The campus office of institutional research can usually provide information about student credit hours, faculty loads, grade distributions, and so forth. The dean's office can offer comparative budget and salary data. Professional associations and administrators' publications often hold normative data by field. Questionnaires useful for gathering students' and graduates' opinions can be developed or modified from existing examples; mailing lists are usually available through an administrative office, like Development or Alumni Affairs.

The chair should ensure that administrators, students and staff, as well as faculty, are interviewed. Interviews are most productive when well-planned and when answers to specific questions are sought. Although some group meetings are useful, especially with students, individual meetings with all faculty are important.

Interpreting the Information

No matter how much quantifiable data are collected, human judgment prevails. Productive interpretations of the data will result from the quality of the questions asked, the experience of the people undertaking the evaluations, and the imaginative use of comparisons to give meaning to the numbers. Two sorts of comparisons should be used whenever possible: comparisons with other units within the institution and comparisons with similar departments at comparable institutions. Some institutions have a list of other schools they consider their peers; in such instances, comparisons of the department with those of the peers is most important.

Writing the Reports

The department assumes responsibility for writing the self-study. This study is then circulated to a campus committee or to outside evaluators or both. The extra-departmental evaluators read the self-study, make whatever other inquiries they think important (including, in the case of the outside evaluators, the site visit), and write a final report. Final reports take many forms. The campus review committee may draft a report and send it to the off-campus evaluators for revision. Each reviewer may be assigned a different section of the report to write, with one person charged with smoothing out the prose and producing the final copy. Each reviewer may write an independent report. A single report is efficient, but it may become bland because of the desire of all signers to agree with all parts of it. Multiple reports are often untidy and contradictory, but they are often more provocative.

Summary

Assessment is a form of peer review. Indeed, departmental assessment is analogous in both form and substance to those faculty reviews that result in tenure, promotion, and merit salary increases. Departments, like faculty, must be productive; departments, like faculty, must remain intellectually vital; departments, like faculty, must serve the institution, the students, and the discipline. Departmental reviews, like faculty reviews, represent the best side of America's educational system, for both are based on an academic model that stresses a community of scholars working rationally and democratically for the good of the whole.

CHAPTER 10

Motivating Faculty

James C. McCroskey and
Virginia P. Richmond

People who are capable and productive at doing something else are most likely to be selected to serve as department chairs. Some are excellent researchers. Some are excellent teachers. Some are excellent in providing service to the institution or larger community. Some are excellent in more than one endeavor. Unfortunately, few people are selected chairs because they have demonstrated excellence in fostering the efforts of their peers, a chair's primary task.

One of the most difficult things for many new chairs to accept is that they are judged more on what their colleagues collectively achieve than what they achieve themselves. No matter how hard a chair tries, he or she cannot conduct enough research for an entire department, nor teach with excellence the majority of the department's courses, nor provide quality service to all constituencies. *The chair's primary task is to coordinate and enhance the efforts of the collective faculty.*

Goal-Setting

A chair must develop clear goals for the department. Coordination and enhancement are virtually impossible without

159

first establishing a clear direction. Motivation without direction is little better than no motivation at all.

When establishing goals the chair must consider both long-term and short-term outcomes. Often, to achieve long-term goals, some short-term goals must be sacrificed. To establish a new research program that qualifies for a major, continuing grant, some current research may be postponed. To launch courses for a new program, some current courses may be offered less often. Similarly, achievement of long-term goals may be postponed because of temporary emergencies. Launching a new program may be delayed because sufficient funding is not available without decimating current programs.

We will not dwell longer on the importance of goal-setting. Other chapters in this volume deal with it and whole books are available on this important process. Suffice to say, directing the efforts of faculty is difficult, at best, if one does not know where the efforts must be directed.

Compliance Versus Motivation

Motivating people who are not internally motivated is difficult. Attempting such efforts for small, routine matters misuses a chair's resources. Many daily items deal with institutional procedures. Rules are established and people are expected to follow them. Grades must be turned in by a certain date, paperwork must be completed by a given time, and so on. Most of these routine matters are mundane. People do them because they are "supposed to" not because they "want" to. If something is not done, the goal for the chair is simple: get it done — whether they like it or not. *This is a compliance-centered goal.*

It is important that chairs sort out those things for which only compliance is expected from those where motivation is needed. Compliance is comparatively easy to achieve, at least on small matters, unless there is some larger issue between the chair and a faculty member. Most often, compliance is the objective when a faculty member is not engaging in appropriate behavior readily observable by the chair and/or others. People "comply" even when they would rather not if they know others are watching. On the other hand, people not subject to surveillance generally do what others want only if they are internally driven (motivated). "Motivated" faculty agree to provide assistance to a community group even though it is unpaid and it provides no special recognition. While chairs want "motivated" faculty, often they are lucky to have "compliant" faculty.

Hiring Motivated Faculty

Motivation resides primarily within an individual. Thus, the chair's first task is to hire motivated faculty. This is difficult but not impossible. It involves three steps: (1) attracting motivated applicants; (2) selecting motivated prospects; and (3) recruiting the top prospects.

Attracting Motivated Applicants

The first step in hiring motivated faculty is advertising faculty vacancies. The way a position is advertised often determines what kind of people apply. Advertising rugged mountains, desirable climate, opportunities for sailing, or quality theatre, symphony and sports programs will increase the number of applicants, but not necessarily the number of motivated applicants. As we will note later, virtually all faculty are interested in quality of life issues, not just motivated faculty. *Motivated people are looking for opportunities such as personal growth, recognition, and achievement.* Position advertisements must emphasize these aspects of the position to attract motivated faculty.

Selecting Motivated Prospects

As most people in higher education know, the best predictor of a student's future grade is the student's past grades. A similar rule applies to selecting motivated faculty from a group of prospects. The best predictor of whether one will perform well in the future is that person's past performance. When seeking a person who is motivated to conduct and publish research, the department's main concern should be whether the person has done so previously. It makes no difference whether the person is a new graduate or an old hand, the issue is the same. The best predictor of future publication is past publication. Truly motivated people publish prior to graduation. People not motivated to publish, seldom do. If the department is seeking a person to develop a program, the best predictor is past success at program development. *Motivation usually is very visible in a resume, if one only looks in the right places.*

Recruiting Top Prospects

Identifying motivated people is easier than hiring them. Motivated people usually know what they are looking for, but do not always make their desires clear in correspondence or interviews. It is very important that all available opportunities are made clear, even if some do not seem particularly important for the individual prospect. *Often prospects have unspoken desires.* We recall an instance during an interview with a prospective faculty member that turned the tide. Mention was made that new computers had been ordered for the faculty. This was very important to this applicant because he had a history of negative experiences with mainframe computers and wanted to operate independently. Until this point the subject of computers had not been mentioned.

As important as it is to recruit the best prospects, it is even more important to discourage people who would be unhappy if they were hired. Honesty is the best policy in the hiring process. If a department places a low value on teaching, it is important that applicants who are motivated to excel in their teaching be aware of that. The same goes for research, public service, campus politics, or any other aspect of the position that might attract a motivated person. *There are few, if any, things more discouraging than to find what a person is motivated to do with excellence is not valued by others.*

Influencing Faculty Behavior

Even if one is fortunate enough to have a motivated faculty, they are not motivated to do *everything* the chair would have them do. Thus, much of a chair's time is spent attempting to influence individual faculty members' behavior. This communication process is often referred to as "motivating" faculty, of providing reasons why they should do what the chair wants.

Behavior Alteration Techniques (BATs)

Although many techniques have been developed from which a chair may choose, the following 23 "Behavior Alteration Techniques" (BATs) offer the chair communication strategies to influence faculty members. (See Figure 10.1 for an overview of each technique and examples of the kinds of statements used with each.) No one BAT is the "best" in all circumstances, some work better under certain circumstances.

Table 10.1
Common Behavior Alteration Techniques

Category	Sample Message
1. Immediate Reward from Behavior	You will enjoy it. It will make you happy. Because it is fun. You'll find it interesting. It's a good experience.
2. Deferred Reward from Behavior	It will help you later on in your career. It will prepare you to take a higher level position. It will count in your favor for promotion.
3. Reward from Chair	I will make you "X" if you do. I will make it beneficial to you. I will count it toward your merit evaluation.
4. Reward from Others	Others will respect you if you do. Your students will respect you if you do. Your colleagues will like you for it. The dean will be pleased if you do.
5. Internal Reward: Self-Esteem	You will feel good about yourself if you do. You are the best person to do it. You always do such a good job. You are so good at it.
6. Immediate Punishment from Behavior	You will lose if you don't. You will be unhappy if you don't. You will be hurt if you don't. It's your loss if you don't.

Table 10.1 continued

7. Deferred Punishment from Behavior	It will hurt you later in your career. It will work against you for a promotion. You won't be able to qualify for a higher position.
8. Punishment from Chair	I will punish you if you don't. I will make it miserable for you. I will make sure you are an outcast. I will take away "X" if you don't.
9. Punishment from Others	No one will like you. Your students will make fun of you. Your colleagues will reject you. The dean will be angry with you.
10. Internal Punishment: Guilt	If you don't, others will be hurt. You will make others unhappy if you don't. Your students will be punished if you don't.
11. Positive Chair Relationship	I will like you better if you do. I will respect you. I will be proud of you. It will indicate you are one of my kind of people.
12. Negative Chair Relationship	I will dislike you if you don't. I'll be disappointed in you. I won't be proud of you. I won't like it.
13. Legitimate Chair Authority	Because I told you to. You don't have a choice in this. I'm in charge, not you. I'm the person you answer to. Don't ask; just do it.
14. Legitimate Higher Authority	Do it; I'm just telling you what I was told. It is a rule; I have to do it and so do you. It's a rule; others expect you to do it.
15. Personal Responsibility	It's your obligation. It's your turn. Everyone has to do his or her share. It's your job. Everyone has to pull his or her own weight.
16. Responsibility to Colleagues	Your colleagues need it done. The department depends on you. All your colleagues are counting on you. Don't let us down.
17. Normative Rules	We voted and the majority rules. All your colleagues are doing it. Everyone has to do it. The rest of the department is doing it.

Table 10.1 continued

18. Debt	You own me one. Pay your debt. You promised to do it. I did it last time. You said you would do it this time.
19. Altruism	If you do this it will help your colleagues. Your students will benefit if you do. I am not asking you to do it for yourself, do it for the good of the department.
20. Peer Modeling	Your colleagues do it. Good faculty members do it. Faculty you admire do it. Your friends on the faculty are doing it.
21. Chair Modeling	This is the way I always do it. When I first started out, that is the way I did it. Most people like me do it that way. I used to do it.
22. Chair Expertise	From my experience, it is a good idea. From what I have learned, it is what you should do. This has always worked for me. Trust me; I know what I am doing.
23. Chair Feedback	Because I need to know how well you understand this. To see how well I have explained it to you. It will help you understand your problem areas.

IMMEDIATE REWARD FROM BEHAVIOR

Often the chair attempts to elicit specific faculty behaviors by suggesting that they are inherently rewarding and fulfilling. The rewarding consequences from engaging in the desired behavior are emphasized. This "try it, you'll like it" approach is useful in situations where faculty are reluctant to engage in behaviors that deviate from the "old way" of doing things. This technique is often helpful in developing a trusting relationship between the chair and a given faculty member. The key is to insure the faculty member *is* rewarded for engaging in the new behavior. If the reward is not forthcoming, not only will the behavior be discontinued but the relationship between the chair and that faculty member may be seriously damaged.

DEFERRED REWARD FROM BEHAVIOR

Sometimes the chair attempts to elicit specific faculty behaviors by suggesting that, if certain behaviors are engaged in, rewards will come at a later time, a later date or later in one's career. For example, the chair might ask faculty members to teach an overload one term, assuring them that their load will be reduced later. In this approach the chair can be explicit about the types of rewards that will come later or they might be inferred. While this technique is not immediately reinforcing, more mature faculty recognize that many rewards are not immediate, but come later in their careers (e.g., working hard early in one's career can have payoffs at a later time).

REWARD FROM CHAIR

This technique is straightforward and clear cut. A chair's influence takes the form of, "If you do this for me, I'll do X for you." This type of reward is usually clear in its orientation: there is a request and an established reward that goes with it. It also is clear the chair is the one granting the reward, not someone else. While this technique can be used occasionally, its impact diminishes if used too often. Chairs realize very early in their careers that they possess a limited number of rewards, rewards better saved for very special situations. This type of influence is often seen as a "bribe." If used too often, a chair will find faculty replying to the request, "What will you do for me if I comply with your request?" Thus, our advice is not to use this technique too often.

REWARD FROM OTHERS

The chair using this technique to elicit a behavior might suggest that "Others will respect you if you do this," or "Your colleagues will like you for this." In this situation the faculty member does something because others (such as colleagues) will be pleased and, as a result, provide him or her some kind of reward. The "others" need not be colleagues. They could be more senior administrators, students, community members, granting agency evaluators, or any other individual or group in a position to provide reward.

INTERNAL REWARD: SELF-ESTEEM

Often a chair attempts to elicit desired behaviors by making the faculty feel good about themselves. This technique centers on people feeling good about themselves for engaging in a desired behavior. The chair might say "You are so good at it," "Only a few people can do such a good job on this" or "You are the best person to do it." This technique usually appeals to a faculty member's better side. It implies that he or she is a worthwhile member of the faculty, capable of making an important contribution. One caution in this regard: this technique works best with faculty who have *high* self-esteem. It validates their own self-perceptions. In contrast, faculty members with *low* self-esteem may be suspicious of such suggestions, seeing the effort as an attempt to "con" them.

IMMEDIATE PUNISHMENT FROM BEHAVIOR

The chair attempts to elicit faculty behavior by suggesting that if the desired behavior is not performed, or some inappropriate behavior is performed, there will be an immediate punishment or loss of some type. This is the flip side of immediate reward from behavior. While immediate reward is dependent upon immediate reinforcement, immediate punishment from behavior is dependent upon some immediate negative outcome. While this technique might be implicit, it often is explicit. For example, a chair might say "If you do X, you will not receive a raise" or "If you don't do X, then you will have to spend all weekend in meetings with colleagues." Note that in both examples, the chair does not say he or she will withhold a raise or force meetings. These negative outcomes are projected as coming from certain behavior choices immediately and automatically.

DEFERRED PUNISHMENT FROM BEHAVIOR

Sometimes the chair attempts to elicit specific faculty behaviors by suggesting that if the behaviors are not engaged in, there will be punishment(s) or losses that will occur at a later time, later date or later in a faculty member's career. This is the flip side of deferred reward from behavior. Its negative impact is not immediate but an implied or explicit threat for the future is used. For example, to get a faculty member to publish more research the chair may say (or write) "If you do not conduct and publish more research you will not be retained in this Department." Or, to encourage a faculty member to be more careful in grading, "The amount of time it takes to check your grades is nothing compared to the amount of time it takes to deal with one irate student or dean."

Most chairs can count the number of times they have clearly stated — or put in writing — what is expected of a faculty member and what the negative consequences will be if the standard is not met. However, faculty often ignore these warnings because the punishment is "down the road" in their professional careers. These same faculty are then "shocked and surprised" to learn they have been denied tenure because their performance was below expectation. Thus, chairs should not expect too much from this technique. People are told not to smoke or they will get lung cancer; they are told to wear seat belts or they will be injured or killed in auto accidents. But people still smoke and ride with belts unfastened. Both insecure and highly future-oriented people respond well to this technique. But most simply do not believe the threat is real until the punishment is immediate.

PUNISHMENT FROM CHAIR

To get faculty to engage in specific behaviors the chair suggests that the faculty will be punished if the request is not complied with. For example, the chair might say, "I will punish you, if you don't do X" or "I will not recommend you for a raise if you don't do X." This technique requires the chair's request to be very clear. In other words, the faculty defying the chair using this technique knows he or she is going to get whatever the chair can mandate as a punishment. As with reward from chair, punishment from chair should be clear, direct, and from the chair, not some other source. Chairs using this technique must be able to institute the punishment; they must also realize that frequent use of this technique destroys relationships.

This type of influence rarely yields more than compliance and often leads to an ineffective relationship between chair and faculty member. However, there are times when a chair may have limited ways to deal with a particular faculty member. If a faculty member is unmotivated, immature, or constantly challenging the chair's authority, then the chair may have to resort to punishment.

PUNISHMENT FROM OTHERS

The chair using this technique to elicit desired behaviors from his or her faculty might say things like, "Others will not like or respect you, if you don't do X" or "No one will want to work with you and you might be disliked by not complying." This type of influence implies that others, such as colleagues, will punish the faculty member if he or she does not do what is expected. This is a very threatening type of influence because peers often *do* punish each other for lack of compliance with rules, requests, and other job duties. Thus, this is a very real form of compliance. Although this type of compliance is not motivating, it frequently gets faculty to do given tasks.

INTERNAL PUNISHMENT: GUILT

This technique elicits behaviors by suggesting the faculty member will feel badly because others, such as colleagues and friends, will be hurt, unhappy, or disillusioned if he or she does not comply. This is a commonly used influence strategy. For example, parents use it with children, saying things like, "How will your Dad feel if you bring home an

'F' in mathematics?" College professors use it, "How will your parents feel when you take home an 'F' in communication?" Department chairs also use this strategy, saying things like, "How will your colleagues react when they hear you didn't do what they were doing?" Or, "How will the co-authors of your convention paper feel when they find out you aren't going to the convention?" The chair might even imply that others will be hurt or punished for lack of compliance. This strategy works well with insecure faculty and those with a high need for approval from their colleagues. More self-confident and less sensitive faculty often care little about how others view them. Thus, a chair must use this technique sparingly and with considerable care.

POSITIVE CHAIR RELATIONSHIP

Sometimes certain faculty behaviors can be elicited by suggesting that the faculty member will be better liked and respected by the chair if certain expectations are met. The chair might say things like, "I will respect you, if you do X" or "I really like people who do X." This technique is particularly useful in compliance gaining because it is based on *referent power.* It assumes that faculty want the respect and liking of their chairs and willingly comply with reasonable requests to gain the chair's respect. Many times a faculty member not only complies with the chair's request, but actually identifies with and internalizes it.

NEGATIVE CHAIR RELATIONSHIP

The chair attempts to elicit certain faculty behaviors by suggesting the faculty member will lose the chair's respect and liking if certain expectations are not met. This is the flip side of positive chair relationship. The chair might say, "I will lose respect for you if you don't do X" or "I don't respect faculty members that do X." This is negative use of referent power. As with its positive use, many faculty comply with the chair's requests to avoid losing his or her respect.

LEGITIMATE CHAIR AUTHORITY

The chair using this technique suggests that he or she has the "legitimate right" as chair to ask faculty members to comply with certain requests or demands. This form of influence stems from the institution assigning chairs the responsibility for enforcing institutional "rules." For example, a chair has the right to request that faculty members teach a certain number of courses, perform duties in a professional manner, and be in attendance at faculty meetings. However, he or she does not have the right to mandate clothing styles or lifestyles. While this form of influence is not perceived as negatively as punishment, its impact is often equally negative. This occurs when a chair relies too heavily on the fact that he or she is the boss and overemphasizes that role. There are some chairs who take assigned authority to extremes, becoming "little Hitlers."

This type of compliance seeking is often seen in memos or departmental meetings where the chair sets forth expectations for faculty to follow. Examples include: "Anyone planning to be out-of-town and miss a class must file Absence Form B before leaving campus." "Please complete a 'delete form' on any student not present on the first day of classes." As can be seen, use of legitimate supervisor authority is grounded in routine matters. When it is extended into more important aspects of a faculty member's life, the chair may encounter substantial resistance.

LEGITIMATE HIGHER AUTHORITY

A chair using this influence strategy suggests the faculty should do what the chair asks, not because of his or her own authority, but because both the chair and the faculty are expected to comply with the requests of a higher authority, such as a dean or provost. For example, chairs and faculty are expected to complete annual personnel reports and return them to a higher source, such as a dean. In most cases, faculty will comply with higher authority *if the request is reasonable*. However, if the requests are unreasonable, the faculty find ways not to comply. Then the higher authority has to try another strategy to get compliance — or delegates the problem to the chair for solution.

PERSONAL RESPONSIBILITY

With this technique the chair attempts to elicit faculty behaviors by pointing out that "Everyone has to do his or her share," "It's your turn" or "It's your responsibility." This obligatory strategy usually leads to compliance with the request without negative feelings because the faculty can see that others have done "their share." In many institutions, this technique is employed through the use of "position descriptions." These instruments enumerate the responsibilities of each individual. Thus, if some responsibility is not being met, the chair has easy access to the "it's your responsibility" claim.

RESPONSIBILITY TO COLLEAGUES

Sometimes faculty behaviors can be elicited by suggesting that the faculty member's colleagues are depending on his or her compliance and responsibility. Few faculty members want to be responsible for their department missing out or not sharing in possible rewards because someone did not "carry his or her load." To influence the faculty member, the chair might say, "Your colleagues need this done, they are depending on you" or "You'll let the group down if X isn't done." This could apply to a number of situations. For example, if a group of faculty are writing a grant proposal, each has a responsibility to the overall group to do his or her share so that the proposal can be finished.

NORMATIVE RULES

The chair using this strategy to elicit faculty behavior depends on majority rule, or the idea that the faculty member should conform because colleagues are following certain behavior patterns. For example, "We voted and the majority rules," "All of your colleagues are doing X," "The entire group is doing X, hence you need to go along with the group." Many times, if the requests are reasonable, faculty conform to the demands because of the norms. Often it is easier to comply with the norm than resist it.

DEBT

A chair may elicit certain behaviors by suggesting that a faculty member "owes" it to the chair to perform some task. Perhaps the chair has done some favors or granted some requests and is "calling in a debt." People often do favors for others, and then expect the favor to be repaid: "I took your class while you were ill, would you attend this meeting for me?" This strategy works well if not abused or used too often. However, overuse leads to strong resentment.

ALTRUISM

The chair using this strategy to elicit faculty member behavior is suggesting that compliance will be beneficial to others, that others will be happier or better off in some way because of the faculty member's behavior. Of course, the faculty member has to want to make others' lives better, such as wanting to make classes more conducive to learning. This strategy works well with some faculty and has little or no impact on others. Some faculty do not have an altruistic "bone in their bodies," while others are very altruistic. A chair can usually tell the difference. For example, the faculty member who insists on creating an impossible learning environment, will not do extra tasks to improve the work environment, and constantly complains about his or her students and colleagues is unlikely to be swayed by altruistic appeals. Whereas the person who is willing to redesign classes for optimal learning, and work with students and other faculty is more likely to be altruistic. Therefore, a chair needs to know his or her faculty well before using this strategy.

PEER MODELING

At times the chair attempts to elicit behaviors by suggesting that a faculty member should comply because friends, colleagues, and admired others are already engaging in the behaviors. For example, the chair might say, "People you respect and like are doing X," or "Others like you are doing X, perhaps you should try it." This is a very appealing form of compliance because people generally try what their trusted friends and colleagues feel is best. Much of the literature on opinion-leadership suggests that an individual is most influenced by people he or she respects and likes. Thus, this is a very potent strategy. Additional reinforcement is present for compliance because colleagues reinforce the faculty member for doing what they are already doing.

CHAIR MODELING

A chair using this technique to influence a faculty member's behavior is suggesting that the faculty person should comply because the chair is engaging in the behavior and the behavior is one the chair thinks is important. The chair might suggest that "this is the way I usually do X" or "people who are like me do it this way." The chair might even suggest "real-life" models that he or she respects, likes, and even models herself or himself as a means of getting a faculty member to engage in appropriate professional behaviors. This strategy will work well if the chair is liked and respected by his or her faculty members. It will not work at all if the chair is disliked or is not respected by her or his faculty members.

CHAIR EXPERTISE

A chair attempts to elicit certain faculty behaviors by suggesting faculty compliance with his or her request because of the chair's expertise and experience in the area. Statements like "I have found this to be the best way" or "From my experience, this usually is the best thing to do" represent use of this technique. If pressed, the chair can substantiate his or her claim by discussing why certain requests are desirable and others are not. This is a very effective means of influencing faculty, particularly if they were originally hired by the same chair. Many times faculty members take positions in a department because of the chair or because of the faculty the chair has hired. This often implicitly speaks to the chair's perceived expertise.

CHAIR FEEDBACK

This technique centers on faculty behaviors that the chair might reasonably be expected to observe and provide advise or assistance in his or her role as an administrator. Such influence attempts are characterized by comments such as " ... so I can see if this will work" or " ... so that I can see if you need some assistance." Chairs often use this technique to help in their supervisory role. Sometimes it is used as an excuse for the faculty member to do the chair a small "favor." By "trying" the requested behavior as a favor, the faculty member may find that it is one to his or her liking and continue it.

Strategies

None of the Behavioral Alteration Techniques is a guaranteed method of influencing faculty behavior. Their potential usefulness varies sharply from situation-to-situation. Any one of the methods loses its value through overuse. It is very important, therefore, that the chair recognize the wide array of techniques available to better adapt to both the individual faculty member and to the particular situation.

It is also important for the chair to recognize that any motivation for behavior change produced by the BATs is likely to be transient. *The techniques are more likely to produce movement than motivation.* Such movement, or short term compliance, is not to be disparaged. Most of needed or desired changes in faculty behavior are of the smaller, transient variety. Motivation is an individual internal state. To produce larger, more long-term behavioral changes involves producing changes in the long-term motivational state of the individual. Producing such change is a much more complex process, one that requires an understanding of the nature of human motivation.

The work of Frederick Herzberg, under the rubric of "motivator-hygiene theory," has provided valuable insight into the complexities of motivation in the workplace.[1] While this overall theory has not been fully supported through research, its main tenets provide insight which is particularly helpful to department chairs. Of prime importance is the recognition that factors facilitating and inhibiting motivation may co-exist. In the following sections we consider each factor.

Permitting Motivation to Surface — Inhibiting Factors

It is difficult to be highly motivated if one is miserable. Such a situation is analogous to having a pebble in a shoe. Most people, try as they might, cannot focus on anything except that pebble until it is removed. All of the problems, all the hopes and aspirations, everything becomes secondary to that irritating pebble. This feeling represents the essence of what we mean by "inhibiting" factors; factors that do not relate to motivation directly. Rather, they are the "pebbles in the shoe" that do not allow motivation.

In academia, these inhibiting factors are elements that make a faculty member dissatisfied. Again, consider the pebble. If the pebble is removed, it is not some wondrous, exhilarating experience; there is temporary relief that it is gone, then the mind moves onto something else. That something else could well be another irritant. The important point to remember is that *an irritant's removal produces no more than momentary pleasure.* It removes dissatisfaction. It does not produce motivation. However, it produces a situation where motivation is a possible outcome, if other circumstances are supportive.

Some of the inhibiting factors that prevent motivation from surfacing in an academic environment include: salary, job security, work conditions, institutional policies and administration, interpersonal relations with the chair, peers, and subordinates, and personal life.

SALARY

When faculty think of job satisfaction, one of the first things coming to mind is salary. On the surface at least, most people think they would be satisfied making a certain amount of income, usually substantially more than currently made. They think that if they could get a raise, they would be happy. While there probably is such a thing as "enough money," it is not something most people are going to have, particularly those in academia. Raises are somewhat like meals. Just because I received one today, do not expect me to turn one down tomorrow. Receiving a significant raise temporarily removes dissatisfaction with salary. However, that dissatisfaction is likely to come back again, often very soon. Since salary is so closely associated with having the "good things in life," pressure to increase salary is a constant irritant.

JOB SECURITY

People who worry about having a job tomorrow cannot be expected to be motivated to perform quality work today. For this reason unions and employee rights have come into existence. Higher education has a unique form of job security called "tenure." Tenure is the goal of almost all young faculty. Once tenure is achieved, or so untenured faculty think, one has "made it." Academic institutions have established tortuous systems which untenured faculty must go through to achieve tenure. Untenured faculty argue they do not have time to be motivated to do anything except achieve tenure. After that is accomplished, so the story goes, the real work begins. Of course, once tenure is granted, the world does not automatically become a wondrous place. Rather, in short order, the issue of tenure fades and other problems are confronted. Another pebble has been removed. On to other irritants.

WORKING CONDITIONS

Working conditions relate to the environment where faculty work. Such basic things as temperature, lighting, size, and comfort come to mind. Generally working conditions are satisfactory unless some environmental element is focused on, rather than on the job. Working in an office that reaches 120° in the summer inhibits motivation, as does having to park a half-mile from the office in a blinding snow storm. Four faculty in a 6' x 6' office tends to block motivation, as does carrying armloads of material across campus while passing dozens of empty classrooms to reach a classroom some clerk decided was the "right" one. All faculty expect reasonable work conditions. If those expectations are not met, motivation will not occur.

INSTITUTIONAL POLICIES AND ADMINISTRATION

Academic institutions are bureaucracies. Some are enormous, larger than moderate-sized cities. Nevertheless, they are created to facilitate the efforts of faculty and students. All policies and administrative efforts are presumably directed toward that objective. When things are going as they should, faculty are hardly aware of the bureaucracy. When they are not, faculty and the bureaucracy often go to war. It is critical that policies and the administration of those policies not interfere with the faculty's day-to-day efforts. When faculty and bureaucrats are in conflict, motivation drops to zero.

INTERPERSONAL RELATIONSHIPS

Faculty expect positive relationships with their chair, colleagues and students. This expectation is not always met, and when it is not, the conflict that arises often overshadows faculty motivation.

PERSONAL LIFE

A faculty member's personal life is not left at home. It goes to work, particularly if there is a problem in it. While personal problems may not be caused by what occurs on the job, those problems often profoundly impact on that person's work. While it is obvious that one could not expect high motivation from a faculty member who has a child dying of cancer, it is less obvious that motivation may be no higher for a faculty member who recently lost an election to some office. The personal life of a faculty member is just that, personal. However, personal problems may make motivation at work impossible.

INHIBITING FACTORS AND THE CHAIR

Given all of these inhibiting factors, it is reasonable to wonder if anyone can be motivated in the academic workplace. Yet we know that highly motivated people *do* exist. In many cases, if it were not for an effective chair, however, such motivation would not be achieved.

One of the most important tasks a chair has is aiding faculty members in preventing and overcoming these dissatisfaction producing, motivation killing factors. A quick reading of the material above indicates, of course, that no chair can be expected to overcome all of the potential inhibitors that could occur. Nevertheless, a concerned chair can be helpful with many. He or she can help the faculty member develop reasonable expectations for salary adjustments, thus avoiding disappointments. The faculty can be informed (if it is true) that the chair is working to help them gain tenure. The chair can work to establish reasonable policies and to administer them in ways that help rather than hinder faculty effort. He or she can serve as an intermediary when faculty run afoul of policies or procedures. The chair can work to establish positive relationships with the faculty. He or she can serve as a trouble-shooter for problems occurring between faculty members or between faculty and students. Finally, while the chair is not a counselor, it is often possible to direct faculty to people who can provide professional help for personal problems. In short, the chair is in a prime position to help remove barriers to motivation that inhibit faculty achievement. The chair *can* be part of the solution.

Encouraging Motivation to Surface — Facilitating Factors

Now that we have examined the things that can get in the way of developing high levels of motivation, we turn to the facilitating factors, those which truly can be said to motivate people. The following are the more important ones: the work itself, potential for personal growth, recognition, responsibility, achievement, and advancement.

THE WORK ITSELF

The work that faculty members do may be the most motivating factor of all. Often it is interesting, challenging, even inspiring. Few things are more motivating than seeing a student learn an important concept or first see the results of a research project that portend a breakthrough in the field. Such motivators are available to people in few occupations. It might be said that if we can just keep the rest of the world out of the way and allow faculty to be faculty, motivation would be a natural outgrowth of the work itself.

POTENTIAL FOR PERSONAL GROWTH

The first time a person is allowed to teach a class usually is an exciting, motivating expoerience. The 500th time he or she teaches that same class usually is not. Unless constraints are placed on a faculty member, he or she will be motivated to improve his or her teaching or research if for no other reason than to avoid the boredom that can set in otherwise. *Being allowed to grow and change for the better is highly motivating to most faculty members.*

RECOGNITION

While modesty does not permit most people to talk about it, most people like to have their work noticed by others. People want to be recognized when they do things well. If faculty believe they will be recognized, it motivates them to do their best work. While doing a good job is motivating in itself, and becoming better at it motivates people even more, having others notice those efforts takes motivation that extra step higher.

RESPONSIBILITY

Many people are motivated to do better work when they are put "in charge" of that work. While there are exceptions, most people enjoy some control over their environments. When one assumes the responsibility for a task, all of the motivators discussed above are enhanced even more.

ACHIEVEMENT

Being able to achieve something one has not achieved before is very motivating. One of the main reasons people set goals is because they realize pleasure from such achievement. Of course, some people are more motivated to achieve; we refer to these people as having a "high need for achievement." Nevertheless, achievement is motivating even to people who are not high in this need.

ADVANCEMENT

Opportunities for advancement in higher education vary by type and faculty. One may advance by accepting a new position in a more prestigious institution, by being promoted in one's own department or by moving into administration. While some faculty have little desire for any of these types of advancement, most are motivated by the possibility of moving to a higher position or rank in their own department. Thus, care should be taken to give full consideration of the present faculty when positions open in a department before hiring someone from the outside.

FACILITATING FACTORS AND THE CHAIR

The role of chair in facilitating motivation deals primarily with "opening doors." When possible, faculty members should be assigned duties they prefer. They should be allowed to "stretch" themselves into new areas. Their good works should be publicly noticed. They should be allowed to have as much responsibility for their own efforts as possible. They should be encouraged to set realistic goals and be provided assistance, when necessary, to help them achieve those goals. Finally, they should be allowed to advance within the department as opportunities become available.

Summary

To be motivated is as normal as not being motivated. Thus, if a chair has one or more unmotivated faculty members, he or she should look first for possible inhibitors in the environment. Once these are reduced, it is time to begin work on the factors which facilitate motivation. It is vital, however, to keep in mind that motivation must come from within, it cannot be "transplanted." Some people never become motivated toward their work, although they might be motivated to something else, such as a hobby.

Awareness of inhibiting and facilitating factors provide the background for selecting the most appropriate means of influencing faculty (BATs) over time toward self-motivation. The chair must be satisfied that he or she has done all that is reasonable to allow motivation to surface. If chairs could perform miracles, they would hold other positions than chair.

---

1. F. Herzberg, *Work and the Nature of Man* (New York: World Publishing Co., 1966).

CHAPTER 11

External Public Relations: Analysis of Image and Directions for Change

June Kable and
Carla Bennett

9:45   (Saturday) Met with local high school teachers to discuss the department's programs; provided brochures and literature.

3:00   (Monday) Faculty meeting. Agenda: the department's image.

Few academic institutions enjoy the unique privilege of a prestigious external image without concerted public relations efforts. Because of reduced student interest in or qualifications for higher education, competition for students is escalating. Small and medium-sized institutions are actively engaged in selling their strengths. Because of decreased numbers of qualified students and the increased public relations efforts of smaller institutions, larger ones are compelled to follow suit. Competition for private endowments, grants and state funds is becoming increasingly more complex.

Attracting and retaining quality students is a problem faced by all department chairs. A favorable image does not "just happen." Therefore, it is the chair's responsibility to answer the question, "What is our external public image?" It is this image that, if positive, earns rewards: increased budgets; established scholarship; named chairs and professorships; sizeable endowments; and majors actively pursued for graduate programs and/or employment.

Public Relations Systems

Public relations systems are defined according to the degree an organization interacts with its environment. This interaction process is defined as either open or closed (Cutlip, Center and Broom, 1985). *Closed systems* have definable, impregnable boundaries that are incapable of interchange with their environments. The department that operates as a closed system loses sight of its constituencies, has no available feedback and therefore is unsure what image it is projecting. This inability to evaluate the *public* environment and to adapt to change eventually results in program demise.

An *open system*, on the other hand, provides opportunities to respond to environmental changes. Healthy, open departments have an interactive relationship with their environmental entities or publics. These publics have needs, wants and expectations that are met by the department. The department also has its own needs and expectations that are met by these environmental entities. Only through an understanding of these *mutual needs* can a department, under the leadership of the chair, pursue an effective public relations plan.

The problem is that many departments, although believing that they are open and communicate well with their various constituencies, actually operate as closed systems. That is, they assume that "Message sent is message received." Faculty members say, "What more can we do? We send out press releases about departmental accomplishments, we send out a newsletter each year. The message goes out, so there's nothing more we can do." Unfortunately, they have no perception of message effectiveness or relevance; they send messages without any idea of how their perspective publics receive them. *A message sent without feedback — formal or informal — is of no value.*

Relating to publics in an open system involves the process of persuasion. Persuasion here is defined as a complex, continuing, interactive process. In this process, senders and receivers are linked by verbal and nonverbal symbols through which one attempts to influence the other to adopt a change in an attitude or behavior. Change occurs because the persuadee's perception is enlarged or changed. This *interactive-dependency approach* to persuasion is neither persuader nor persuadee-oriented, rather it involves the interaction of both parties (O'Donnell and Kable, 1982). In this process, the department is the persuader and its various publics are the persuadees. Each entity, both persuader and persuadee, has its own goals, needs and expectations that must be met. A successful public relations campaign involves persuasion which seeks and finds a commonality of needs and provides opportunities that are mutually satisfactory to both.

External publics are not a mass audience. Each public must be defined and addressed. Publics are not static, they change as their social environments change. Often, departments assume knowledge of the publics' perceptions of them, but often their information is dated, incorrect and/or greatly limited. *Improving or adjusting an external image is futile until the internal image is understood.* Therefore, a chair needs to (1) identify the various publics that impact on the department; (2) evaluate the internal image projected in the past; and (3) formulate a plan to project a unified external image. This chapter addresses these three processes.

Identification of Publics

Publics are any group of people tied together, however loosely, by some common bond of interest or concern (Newsom and Scott, 1985). Chairs must identify each of the many publics that have ties to or knowledge of their departments. The following are examples of important publics.

Secondary School and Community College Instructors

Information concerning high school and community college instructors in the appropriate discipline(s) is pertinent. Interest in this public includes information about the percentage of their graduates attending the institution and the institutions instructors or teachers recommend to their students. Answers to questions like "What are the strengths of the instructor(s) and the program(s) in each school?" and "What is the counseling philosophy for students desiring a college degree?" provide insights as to directions for targeting this public.

Graduates

Information on all graduates, their locations and their career choices and status provide chairs valuable information as to the strengths and weaknesses of their programs. Providing graduating seniors a simple form that includes permanent addresses and future plans is a good first step for keeping track of departmental graduates. A departmental newsletter provides former students an opportunity to update addresses and contribute news concerning his or her professional progress and keeps records current. This public, if properly motivated and provided with adequate and interesting information, can serve as effective ambassadors for the program.

Professional and Industrial Organizations

Past ties with area professionals or industrial organizations need to be assessed. Past projects that have been mutually beneficial need to be reappraised. For example, if participation in an annual workshop declines over a period of several years, assessment might indicate the problem can be solved with a simple change in format. Mailing lists also need to be updated as the contact people in these groups change. However, targeting any organization simply because "we have always done it" wastes resources and funds. Common goals and mutual needs must underlie the choices of target industries and professional associations as significant publics.

Internships

Many departments engage in relationships with the surrounding community through internship and cooperative education programs. Examples might include an accounting department student setting up a bookkeeping system for a nonprofit organization, a dental hygiene program providing free dental care to the public or a journalism student writing for a local newspaper. All potential community needs that might be met by his or her department should be continually assessed by the chair. An intern interacting with the community demonstrates the department's quality through his or her performance. Minimum grade point average requirements, previous performance in the department and careful screening of internship applicants insure a positive relationship between the student and the community — as well as the department and the community.

Broadcast and Print Media

The media are no longer considered the enemy of management. Informed administrators build bridges between themselves and the press based on the institution's need for exposure and the media's need for information. Personal contact with key media personnel is critical. Credibility, however, is based on an honest relationship and *the importance of establishing credibility with the media cannot be overemphasized.*

Chairs should review past media experiences and relationships so that new avenues of media use can be explored. For example, sending a robot to a television station to announce an upcoming science workshop is preferable to the "old dry news release" sent year after year. Executing creative means of attracting both broadcast and print media insures maximum exposure. The chair should also work with the university relations or public information office to improve media relationships.

Graduate Schools or Potential Employers

With further education, graduates continue to enhance the institution's image. If 100% of pre-med graduates are accepted into medical school or if 30% of mass communication graduates become news directors, the departmental image is enhanced through these impressive numbers. These accomplishments, however, are of no value unless they are effectively disseminated to appropriate publics.

Gathering Feedback

Before communicating with his or her various publics, the chair needs to study the effectiveness of past communications and relationships with these publics. How have past relationships with external publics evolved? How credible is the department with its publics? What feedback has been received concerning past projects? Are there new publics not addressed by the department? These questions must be researched before future plans can be formulated.

Internal efforts at creating and maintaining an external image may prosper through informal feedback from faculty. Additionally, chairs should examine old brochures, news releases and other uses of media, and any promotional efforts already in place. Next, the chair should lead the department in deciding what its image *should be*, not what it thinks or says it is. Cohesiveness of purpose is of utmost importance here and methods for acquiring feedback concerning the image should be initiated.

The most common feedback vehicles are *interviews* and *surveys*. Short, succinct questions that identify departmental strengths and weaknesses are very useful. A theatre department might conduct a short survey at the box office to assess its advertising campaign. A music department might attach a brief questionnaire to all its printed programs. These short surveys yield reliable information as long as the respondents remain anonymous and provide feedback from committed publics, those participating in a departmental event. Personal contact is an important feedback method; however, it should be remembered that interview responses can be biased in many ways. Personal interviews should be collected according to a well-designed survey research plan.

Research also takes the form of logging occasions when news releases find their way into media outlets, as well as determining which media seem to yield the best reviews. Discovering innovative ways of reaching the various media can revitalize a program. A high percentage of press releases that never reach the public, however, require an immediate review of the entire process.

The chair must remember that surveys, telephone interviews or other formal methods of gaining feedback should be short, easily understood and yield a response that is of substantial use to the department. Long and confusing questions and open-ended or "loaded" questions are of little value at this stage of plan development. Therefore, the chair should carefully evaluate his or her faculty when delegating responsibility for creating feedback instruments — or contacting the appropriate institutional office for help.

The open system, with its consideration of *mutual* expectations and use of *feedback*, is an effective system of public relations. The chair's first public relations job is to define the department's publics. Each discipline is challenged to search for its own publics, publics with a vested interest in the education and development of the graduates of that discipline's program.

Effects of Internal Publics on External Publics

A chair must not only be concerned about a consistent departmental image, but must facilitate avenues to project that internal image to external publics. Some administrators analyze internal images and external images, but they almost never examine effects of the internal image on its external publics.

For example, most departments have a "loner" faculty member such as discussed in Chapter One. Suppose this person (a biology professor) is asked by someone in the community, "Are your pre-med students accepted into medical schools?" and he or she answers, "I don't know." This response incurs damage to the institution's external image. While most faculty understand what they need from the external public, they do not understand that inappropriate messages become part of the external public's image of the institution. This image may prohibit the fulfillment of faculty needs. Even thoughtless remarks to a neighbor can have a negative effect on an external public. Each faculty member must understand, contribute to and articulate the mission and goals of the department to external publics. This process of relating to external publics contributes to meeting both their needs and those of their external publics.

The internal public — the department — also affects the external public through messages conveyed via letters to scholarship donors, potential scholarship recipients and their parents, legislators and to members of Boards of Regents. Written communication is another avenue through which a faculty member can either damage or enhance the department's external image. Careful consideration of *content, word choices* and *target audiences* are guidelines for written communications generated by the department. A chair should offer to proofread and approve letters, brochures and news releases before they are sent. Most young and inexperienced faculty members welcome guidance in these efforts.

Other media that help reflect the departmental image include bulletin boards, posters, direct mail and special event programs. A chair is responsible and should consider the department's *overall* potential public relations campaign. As such, all media should be coordinated and consistent with other external media pieces, even if they target a specific audience. Lack of consistency in the form, style and/or color of all external media can blur a department's identity, as well as incur additional expenses.

Faculty also play a significant public relations role by motivating students to pursue excellence. Just as many academic institutions are known to the general public for their sports programs, faculty can help create positive *academic* program images to specific or general publics. This is accomplished when faculty encourage students to enter intercollegiate competitions; participate in workshops; submit and present scholarly papers at state, regional and national conferences; gain acceptance into honor societies; and become involved in student organizations that engage in worthwhile service projects. Each activity gains positive recognition for the department of which the students are a part.

Administrators and faculty often overlook the fact that *the staff* can have a tremendous effect on external publics. Often staff members are approached to get the "inside" story on a development within the institution. The staff member's message has credibility whether he or she is informed or not. Moreover, when staff do not understand the departmental mission, potential ambassadors are lost. Articulating their importance and contributions to the department's public relations efforts has several positive benefits. It builds morale in secretaries who answer telephones and need to be informed, in custodians who are frequently stopped in the hall and asked for information and in graduate students or teaching assistants and adjunct faculty who often feel like departmental "stepchildren."

Chairs must remember and stress that the internal departmental image does not operate exclusively within its own boundaries. Faculty, staff and students all significantly affect the external image. Only when the department is aware of this fact is it time to prepare an external public relations plan conveying the image the department wishes to project.

Creating and Conveying the External Image

Armed with a realistic internal image and all pertinent research data, the chair and faculty can investigate new vehicles for reaching external publics. A unified vision of a department's goals and mission should be evident in the projects and programs chosen for specific audiences. Faculty, staff and administrators should participate in both short- and long-range goal formulation. Based on the agreed-upon image, the department should choose themes, slogans and other strategies consistent with achieving that image. Each strategy should have a specific goal or outcome projected to facilitate later evaluation and assessment.

For example, if research shows that secondary school teachers have little or no knowledge of the department, an "open house" might be staged geared to that audience. If their information is dated, all secondary teachers could be placed on a mailing list for a brochure detailing the latest equipment or processes used by the department and the discipline. A "careers day" project demonstrating current and future career options is of interest to most parents and students. Often they can be staffed by students and alumni who can provide both expectations and real world experiences, as well as the faculty.

Many academic institutions are perceived as remote and separate from the community. Efforts to change this perception should be institution-wide, but a department can still establish its own plans to change its community image. For example, joint sponsorship with appropriate community groups of science fairs, cholesterol screenings or art gallery openings are all appropriate ways to demonstrate involvement with the various publics. A community orchestra, band or choir organized by a music department is often a successful "town-gown" project. This campus/community setting creates an impetus for the campus academic programs as well. However, chairs should remember to clear any such projects with senior administrators. This not only insures that departmental plans fit the institution's plans, but also serves to enhance the department's image with senior administrators.

A trend today is for industries and institutions of higher education to become partners in the educational process. Properly-trained and knowledgeable graduates are vital in today's highly-specialized industries. A research project jointly sponsored by the department and a local industry or municipal agency are examples that meet the mutual needs of both the department and the external public. For example, a chemistry student or faculty member might be retained by a corporation or municipal water works department to design a strategy for a waste water treatment center. The project would assure compliance with Environmental Protection Agency standards. As a result, good will is created and the department's image makes the statement that it is responsive to changing needs in the workplace or community.

Ribbon-cutting ceremonies or news conferences, with appropriate press packets touting new or expanding facilities are excellent opportunities for establishing good media relations. Chairs should notify the media well in advance with an organized and detailed account of the activities planned. Scheduling events when the media can "make deadline" and supplying excellent press packets with all pertinent information results in increased media coverage.

Providing the media with feature stories and accompanying photographs that spotlight talents, accomplishments or honors received by various faculty members keeps the department in the public eye. Other possible "image builders" include: fairs, festivals or receptions, training programs, announcement of special awards or sponsorship of special events. Also, showcasing outstanding student awards and accomplishments provides further exposure for the department. When this information is sent to the student's local newspaper, the department's target population is broadened. On most campuses, this type of information is handled by the public information or relations office, but effective chairs not only make sure the information reaches that office in time for it to be considered current by the media but also makes sure it is communicated in the appropriate format for the particular public(s) targeted. Each function should satisfy a defined public with a specific goal and each occasion should reflect the department's image.

Summary

For an effective public relations plan, the chair must identify the publics, establish a realistic internal image and launch a campaign to reach those publics with the desired image. This chapter has suggested several possible publics, offered suggestions for successful departmental interaction with those publics and presented viable directions for change.

In an active and vibrant department, searching for feedback is a constant process. An open communication system suggests that since images are never constant, research is never complete. As external publics change their attitudes, beliefs and priorities, so must a department change in its public relations philosophy and approach. Effective long-range planning insures that change is not suddenly thrust on a department, but consists of a small series of "image refining" shifts taking place over time.

These new directions for change need not incur additional expense. Public relations practitioners suggest that long-range planning and consistent external projections will probably be cost-saving, as efforts are not duplicated or aimed at unprofitable audiences.

An institutional image is a combination of what an institution does, what it says it does and what people believe it to be (Levinson, 1966). When the department's internal and external publics images are similar, then departmental identity is clear. Any department whose identity is unclear, however, will have difficulty competing for top students in today's competitive environment. When successful persuasion has occurred through an open system of public relations, then the department's expectations have been met. Its publics, as a result, perceive their relationships with the department as vital, ongoing and rewarding. Success comes from a relationship of mutual satisfaction.

References

Cutlip, S., Center, A., and Broom, G. (1985). *Effective public relations*. Englewood Cliffs, NJ: Prentice–Hall.

Levinson, H. (1966). How to undermine an organization. *Public relations journal, 22,* 10, 82–84.

Newsom, D., and Scott, A. (1985). *This is PR: The realities of public relations*. Belmont, CA: Wadsworth.

O'Donnell, V., and Kable, J. (1982). *Persuasion: An interactive-dependency approach*. New York: Random House.

Appendix A
Acquiring Information

Mark Hickson III,
Don W. Stacks, and
Randall K. Scott

Information Needed by a New Chair

There are seven categories of information basic to any chair:

1. Personnel records of faculty and staff.
2. Budget information from current and past years.
3. Departmental data on majors, graduates, alumni, etc.
4. Advising procedures.
5. General policies and procedures.
6. Facilities and allocations.
7. Schedule information.

Personnel

Generally, there are three *formal* channels (written documents) that provide personnel information. These include departmental records, dean's records and records at the personnel office. The following specific types of data are needed:

(1) date the person was hired; (2) current rank and salary; (3) tenure and promotion status; and (4) evaluation reports. All this information *should be* easily accessible in a departmental file. If a departmental file does not contain an updated curriculum vitae, the new chair should request one. Faculty salary records could also be beneficial and are obtainable from the personnel office. Faculty should have an opportunity to review and verify these files annually.

In most instances, information acquisition is simply an updating of current personnel files. In this process, the faculty or staff member should be provided periodical access to his or her file. Unnecessary information, particularly *kudos* and complaints that were dismissed twelve months or earlier should be removed from the file, given to the faculty member involved or destroyed.

Sometimes, a personnel file must be created. The file is set up in an orderly fashion and *contains only the information needed by the chair to make subsequent decisions.* Once the chair has all the formal information needed, informal information is gathered. Early interviews with each faculty member are beneficial to provide the chair with the faculty member's *perception* of status. This information, however, should not become part of an official file. Student complaints and other actions against the faculty member should be explained. If action was taken, and if that action required the information to remain in the file, it should remain. *All unsubstantiated allegations should be periodically reviewed and destroyed.*

Budget

Often fiscal years are not consistent with calendar years or academic years. Moreover, universities may set different dates for their fiscal year. For this reason, the new chair needs two years' budget figures. The sources of information include, but are not limited to, records maintained in the department, dean's office, research office, development office and financial aid office.

The departmental secretary should keep information on the allocations as well as expenditures. The chair needs to know what the various accounts are and whether they are restricted for use in a single area or for a single purpose. For example, a new chair needs office equipment, can the money be taken from "the equipment" account? Better still, will the dean's office or another office on campus pay for it?

The places where additional accounts and/or monies are available to the department include scholarship funds, monies for summer teaching or research, monies from the graduate school, monies from the alumni association and other sources. In the case of scholarship money, information may be found in the department. Sometimes information is found in the development office, the dean's office or the graduate office (especially for fellowships). Sometimes these monies are part of a grant. The departmental secretary may be aware of some or all of these sources of scholarships. The chair must, however, attempt to discover additional sources when possible. The research office or the graduate school may have summer salary money for research or for new course development. Alumni associations often provide funds for newsletters and provide computerized mailing lists. Sometimes the dean's office has allocations for special departmental projects.

The chair also needs to discover endowment funds and determine how they are to be used. What latitude does the chair have in allocating these funds? Is only the interest available? And, if so, at what time of the year? (Often endowment funds are on a different schedule than the institutional fiscal budget.)

The chair needs to know the institution's budget-making process. To what extent does the chair influence salary increases? Are there union restrictions? Merit increases? How is merit determined?

Student Information

The chair needs student data ranging from high school applicants to alumni. Generally, the following types of data should be retained:

1. Number of people who have requested and been given information about the department, as well as names,

addresses, phone numbers and American College Test
(ACT) or Scholastic Aptitude Test (SAT) scores and high
school records, if available. (These statistics indicate the
amount of interest in the department's course of study
and program.)

2. Number of majors and demographic information on
   each. (These data can be compared to those of other
   departments.)
3. Number of credit hours generated during the previous
   year.
4. Number of majors who have graduated each year.
5. Number of honor graduates each year.
6. Names, addresses and telephone numbers of departmental alumni. (This information should be accessible
   through the college/university's alumni office.)

These data will vary considerably from department to department. Some departments have as few as five majors, while
others have several hundred. The larger the number of majors,
the more difficult the information is to obtain and maintain.
If there have been evaluations of the department which
included alumni or majors' responses, the chair should obtain
them. These data often reveal subjective judgments for future
reference.

Student and alumni records require constant attention.
Names change because of marriage and divorce. Addresses
constantly change. Students change majors into, out of, and
back into the department. A computerized data base helps
when the numbers are large.

Advising

Advising procedures are usually published and the col-
lege/university catalog and are a good starting place to
acquire advising information. However, issues arise when
students' wish to change advisors, as well as when faculty
wish students to change advisors. Most faculty would like to
advise between four to ten National Merit scholars and no
one else. Unfortunately, such cases are rare. The chair must
determine how advisors are assigned, keeping in mind that
faculty will complain of having too many — as well as too

few — advisees. Generally, this can be alleviated with a workload policy (to be discussed later). What the chair needs to know *now* is: (1) Who is the student supposed to see? (2) What are the chair's advising responsibilities? (3) What are the graduation requirements? (4) Who can waive a requirement? (5) Who decides what credits may be transferred? And, (6) who certifies the student for graduation?

Policies and Procedures

Most universities have policy and procedure manuals. At a minimum, most have a student catalog and a faculty/staff handbook. The new chair should read these resources, preferably before becoming the chair. Some institutions are even more explicit and have policy and procedure manuals for the various offices, the colleges and schools and perhaps departments as well. What should be included in a departmental policy and procedure manual? Depending on the nature of the department, such a document might not be necessary. For example, a three-person department might not need such a manual, while a larger department would. Size, however, is not the only important factor. If there are seven *different* majors in a department of twelve people, a manual might be needed for faculty advising. Generally, a policy and procedure manual should contain the following:

1. Basic definitions.
2. Evaluation criteria.
3. Tenure and Promotion statements (university, school or college and departmental).
4. Decision-making process.
5. Teaching policies (syllabi, gradebooks/disks, curricula, textbook orders, curriculum change procedures, attendance policy, faculty evaluations by students, overload teaching policy, final examinations policy and any legal concerns involved in teaching [Academic Freedom, Buckley Amendment, etc.], end of semester and end of year checklists).
6. Outside consulting policy.
7. Travel authorization and reimbursement.
8. Staff policies.

9. Faculty and staff benefits information.
10. Policy on outside fund raising.
11. Policy on equipment.
12. Budget information.
13. Planning calendar.

This list is not intended to be all inclusive. However, the most important factors are probably definitions and information about the decision-making process. For example, does the faculty simply make *recommendations* to the chair? Who can vote? What is the meaning of a faculty vote? On what topics do faculty vote? Who is authorized to spend money? Who decides on new faculty job descriptions? How are positions allocated *within* the department? How are offices allocated? The more specific the question, the less likely it should be included in a policy and procedures manual. The *issues* for the manual are: (1) What is the departmental philosophy? (2) What general methods implement this philosophy?

Facility Allocation

Most universities and colleges have limited space. The new chair needs to know how much space the department is allocated — for laboratories, for classrooms, for offices, etc. In addition, the chair needs to determine how space is reallocated. Once the chair knows what space is available, a determination of use and efficiency is needed. The new chair should recognize, however, that the allocation of office space is a very controversial decision. Later in this book we will discuss how the chair deals with such controversial topics to minimize both chair and faculty stress.

Scheduling

Scheduling is another controversial topic. Many faculty are only concerned about their own courses and the times and places of their own classrooms. Others are concerned that students can take the courses necessary to graduate. Of necessity, the chair must be concerned about the student's views too. Faculty convenience is not always possible. From the beginning, the new chair should make this point clear

To his or her faculty. Many departments have an assistant chair or some other faculty who schedules classes. *Ultimately, however, scheduling responsibility rests with the chair.*

Table 1.1
The Chair's Files

1. Policies and procedures

1.1 University policies and procedures
    1.1.1 Faculty handbook
    1.1.2 Memoranda
    1.1.3 Policy and procedures manuals

1.2 School/College policies and procedures

1.3 Departmental policies and procedures
    1.3.1 Definitions (rank, etc.)
    1.3.2 Departmental governance
    1.3.3 Evaluation criteria
        1.3.3.1 Annual evaluation
        1.3.3.2 Salary formulae
        1.3.3.3 Tenure
        1.3.3.4 Promotion
    1.3.4 Teaching policies and procedures
    1.3.5 Other personnel procedures
    1.3.6 Budgetary information (process)
    1.3.7 Annual planning calendar

2. Personnel records

2.1 Names, social security numbers

2.2 Other demographic data

2.3 Curriculum vita

2.4 Date of hiring

2.5 Rank, salary, tenure status

2.6 Evaluation reports
    2.6.1 Annual reviews
    2.6.2 Salary history
    2.6.3 Tenure reports, letters, etc.
    2.6.4 Promotion reports, letters, etc.

Table 1.1 continued

3. Student records

    3.1 Names, social security number, address, telephone number

    3.2 Other demographic data (especially for affirmative action)

    3.3 Hours completed

    3.4 Graduation date

    3.5 [Switch to Alumni records]
        3.5.1 Names, social security number, address, etc.
        3.5.2 Other demographic data
        3.5.3 Major, minor, area of specialization
        3.5.4 Date of graduation
        3.5.5 Placement information (employer, graduate school, etc.)

4. Advising procedure

5. Budget

    5.1 Annual allocation
        5.1.1 Salaries and wages
        5.1.2 Equipment
        5.1.3 Supplies
        5.1.4 Travel
        5.1.5 Scholarships
        5.1.6 Other (including endowments, other budgets)

    5.2 Annual expenditures
        5.2.1 Salaries and wages
        5.2.2 Equipment
        5.2.3 Supplies
        5.2.4 Travel
        5.2.5 Scholarships
        5.2.6 Other

6. Facilities and other non-budgetary allocations

7. Schedule information (including annual schedule of classes; procedure)

Accessing Information

There are two basic means by which information is developed, exchanged, and processed in an academic system. Most universities and colleges incorporate some of each. Some, however, are one-sided, one way or the other. For this reason we focus on the institution's *oral culture* and its *bureaucracy*.

Table 1.2
Acquiring Information

Type of Data	*Sources*	*Frequency*
Personnel	Personnel Office Department Dean	Continuous Minimally annual
Students	Admissions Faculty Registrar's Office Institutional Research	Continuous Minimally term
Alumni	Alumni Office	Annual
Policy/Procedure	V-P for Academic Affairs Dean Business Office Personnel Office [Possibly: President's Office; Board Office; V-P for Research; V-P for Adminstration]	Continuous
Advising	Dean Department V-P for Academic Affairs [Possibly: V-P for Student Affairs]	Annual
Budget	Business Office Department Dean Financial Aid Development Office Research Office	Continuous
Facilities	Dean V-P for Administration Registrar's Office	Annual
Scheduling	Department Dean Registrar's Office Continuing Education	Annual

Timeliness of Information

The chair should think of information as falling into several time frames: (1) the beginning of the job, (2) the beginning of the year, (3) term-by-term data, (4) annual data, (5) 3–5 year data and (6) cumulative data. Most of what was discussed earlier in this chapter can be described as data needed by the chair early in his or her tenure. That is, the information should be acquired by the end of the chair's first term or first year.

Beginning of the Year

Because of faculty turnover each year, it is important for the chair to have a meeting of all full- and part-time faculty at the beginning of a new academic year. Some departments go on "retreats" to undertake these tasks; others cover their start-up meeting as part of a regular departmental meeting. We recommend that the first faculty meeting be about one full day, with a lengthy lunch break for faculty to get to know one another or reacquaint themselves after the summer break.

At this juncture the new chair should focus on information from the view-point of students and faculty. The planning calendar, which is developed for departmental policy and procedures manual should be available to the faculty. Minimally, it should contain dates for (1) preregistration, (2) registration, (3) holidays, (4) institutional and departmental meetings, and (5) conventions or meetings that are usually attended by faculty members. With the planning calendar in place, the chair should then state his or her *expectations* for the year, beginning with the fall term by addressing the following:

1. *At the beginning of the term.* Who has the authority to add students to a class that is already full? What does the faculty do if a student is not on the class roster but shows up after the first week? How can faculty derive information concerning who is supposed to be in class? (the chair should look at this problem from the view of a *new* faculty member.)

2. *During the term.* How will students' complaints be handled? Under what circumstances should a student receive an incomplete grade?

3. *At the end of the term.* Where and when are grades to be delivered? What about posting final grades in the department?

In essence, the new chair should *anticipate* many of the questions that faculty have about grading, syllabi, gradebooks, grades, class attendance and departmental teaching policies.

The new chair should then move on to the year. He or she should emphasize meetings, reports that will be due, end-of-year checkout procedures, requests for travel and requests for supplies. Again, the departmental policy and procedures manual should cover most of these items; however, they should be discussed at the meeting since changes often occur during the year, new faculty need orientation and there may be suggestions for new or revised policies. The chair should suggest a schedule of courses for the *following* year, providing about a month for faculty to recommend changes. Monthly meetings of departmental faculty should be sufficient to update changes during the year.

Three-to-Five Year Data

Three-to-five year data are cumulative. They come from previous years and are useful in evaluating the department, preparing accreditation reports and the like. Some information may be kept more than five years, but data archives are costly both in terms of space and time.

Why Data Collection is Important

By this time, the new chair should have an idea of what *minimal* data are needed. The data discussed provide the basics for managing communication in the academic department. For data to become information, however, *interpretations* of the data must be made. Are there too few majors? Too many? Too few faculty? Too many? Is there a lack of space?

Data collection is the first step in the decision-making process. The use to which the data are put depends upon the department's goals and purposes. Data may be used to argue for additional positions. But what if the administration asks a department to cut back on the number of majors? Then, using the data, a chair could begin developing criteria to limit enrollment (establishing, for instance, minimal grade requirements, new sequences of "cutting" classes, etc.). The data may reveal that some faculty are teaching too few courses or too few students, or that faculty are not balancing research and service with teaching responsibilities. Additionally, the dean's ASAP request for a list of priorities for a $10,000 supplement can be found easily.

The Information-Processing System of the Department

Altogether, then, the new chair must derive data from a number of sources. After collecting the needed data, he or she will have to turn the data into useful information. In this sense, a department chair is primarily an information processor. Requests are made for information about the major, grades, memoranda from various offices, announcements, summaries of institutional data, faculty meetings, student grievances, faculty grievances, kudos from outside agencies and the like. Information is sent out of the department in the form of student recruitment information, faculty recruitment information, grades, lectures, workshops, convention presentations, grant applications, article submissions, book proposals and so forth. The amount of information acquired can quickly become intolerable for a new chair unless communication is managed. Communication cannot be managed via the "hip pocket" approach. All chairs must return telephone calls expeditiously, they must be able to change vocal tones instantly (as in accepting thanks from the garden club president, in explaining to faculty members that their salaries will not be what they expected, in meeting a foreign dignity at a President's reception, to firing a secretary). The new chair faces many problems that practice will solve; however, there are many problems that can be overcome through judicious uses of information.

Appendix B
Providing Information

Don W. Stacks and
Mark Hickson III

Part of a new chair's responsibility is being an information gatekeeper. Chairs constantly process information from one place to another — constantly *communicating* with various audiences or publics. Effective chairs quickly learn to judge the importance of a piece of information and how to transmit it to the *appropriate* receiver. The role of *information provider* places the chair in a precarious situation. First, he or she must understand how information is transmitted — flows — in the institution. Second, the chair must distinguish between information that can be freely distributed, that which is confidential, as well as that which has no use.

The chair is often required to provide similar information to different audiences. There are several ways this is done, each influenced by the institution's dominant culture. In a bureaucracy, information frequently flows downward. Downward information flow is quick; recipients are selected for particular reasons. Bureaucracies also employ lateral (horizontal) and upward flow, but less frequently than downward flow. In an oral culture, information flow is different. The flow of information and how that information is perceived differs between bureaucracies and oral cultures. Each defines "confidentiality" differently. New chairs have to quickly learn how information flows in their institutions, what information is sensitive or confidential and how it should be handled.

Information Flow

Information flow deals with how information is communicated in an organization. The academic institution is no different than any other organization, be it IBM or XYZ Industries. As the organization matures certain predispositions for how information flows emerge. There are two principle forms of institutional communication: bureaucratic and oral culture. While some institutions are one or the other, most possess a little of the characteristics of each. We examine each in turn.

Information Flow in a Bureaucracy

There are three types of information (communication) flow in a bureaucracy (see Figure A.1). Downward communications come from superiors to subordinates, president to dean, dean to faculty, etc. Upward flow is the opposite, subordinate to superior. Lateral or horizontal communication flows between *equals*, dean to dean, chair to chair, etc. Generally, the downward flow is a relatively insignificant problem for a department chair. However, lateral flow (especially within the department and between departments) is a problem. Additionally, upward flow from faculty to the chair can be a problem.

DOWNWARD FLOW

Information flowing downward often deals with changes in institutional policies and procedures arriving from the vice president's office. In this case the chair's first decision is: *Does the faculty need to know this?* In most cases the answer is, "yes." Next, the chair must decide how to let the faculty know.

FIGURE 2.1 INFORMATION FLOW

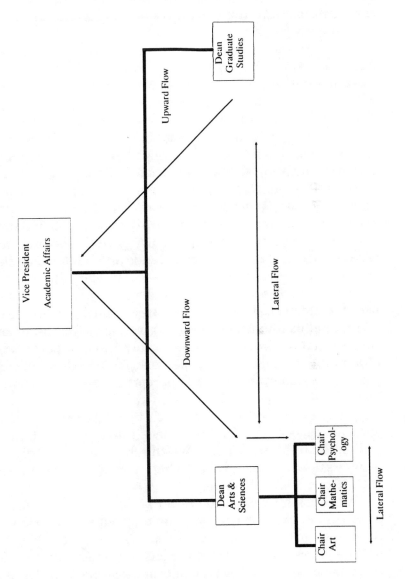

Generally, there are five means of transmitting such information: (1) holding a faculty meeting; (2) providing each faculty a written copy; (3) posting it on a bulletin board; (4) circulating one copy through the faculty; and (5) oral transmission to each faculty.

In a large department, these options are reduced to two: faculty meetings and written copies to all faculty. While such messages will stimulate discussion, resistance, etc., they do not require a response. On the other hand, faculty meetings provide a forum for discussion and should be conducted when the faculty are affected (i.e., smoking, office hours, salary). It may be beneficial to provide a copy to each faculty member before the meeting so that discussion is directed toward the matters at hand. One good principle when thinking about information is: *Redundancy is good.* Because some faculty are good listeners, redundancy will be complained about, made fun of, etc.; the chair should disregard this because, for each faculty member who understands and implements the policies on first notice, there are several who will not.

When possible, the chair should explain *why* a policy is being implemented. For example, strict policies concerning when final examinations may be given are often based on the fact that the institution uses exam periods as part of the total number of minimal days per term for accreditation purposes. It is important that all appropriate people — faculty and staff — receive the information at least twice. Additionally, they should receive it through two *different* channels, with an opportunity for face-to-face interaction so that a rationale can be provided. When the chair disagrees with a policy rationale, it is good to bring in someone who agrees with it to explain the policy.

When communication downward is *initiated* by the chair, he or she needs to consider whether all faculty need to know. If the average faculty member's telephone bill is $25 a month, but one incessant faculty member has an average bill of $150, there is no need to send that information to all faculty. As a second principle, then: *Communicate downward information on a need-to-know basis.* In cases such as this, the chair needs to explain to the individual faculty member that the budget does not allow for these calls. Redundancy may be beneficial here, too. Obviously, there is a misunderstanding about telephone policy if there has been one. It needs to be corrected as soon as possible. Face-to-face interaction might allow the faculty to remind the chair that he or she is the president of a professional association that year. After the conversation, the chair might reach some compromise, such as splitting telephone costs with the association.

Another type of downward information has to do with external messages. External messages are calls for professional papers, employment listings, etc. This information is best provided via a departmental notebook accessible to all faculty. No one is required to read it, but it is available. It should be placed in a convenient location; however, no one is allowed to remove it. This is preferable to having faculty pass the information around; in such a system the information often gets "stuck" on someone's desk. Third-class mail (such as advertisements for books) can be collected in a central location; however, it should specifically be made available to the person(s) responsible for library acquisitions.

A chair's general tendency is to provide *positive* information face-to-face or by telephone and to provide *negative* information in writing. This is not always the best tactic, even though it is the easiest. As a third principle: *Negative information should be redundant.* Written condemnations, however, should be approached with caution and forethought. There are possible legal repercussions for many actions and written documentation may make the chair responsible for them. This is true when negative information is provided in written form, especially when the information is written in a state of anger. A chair should always "count to 10" before writing a reprimand. The chair must ensure that the facts are not only correct, but that the action being taken has true cause. Memoranda or letters written in a state of anger often contain misinformation. The faculty member should know that something negative has happened and that the chair does not like it. It may be best to communicate this dislike face-to-face first and in written form at a later date, especially if this is the second or later occurrence of the problem.

LATERAL FLOW

There are two types of lateral flow important to any chair: within the department and between departments. Within the department flow concerns events, perceptions and policy affecting individual faculty, as well as the department as a whole. For example, faculty often think that they are the only ones doing a significant amount of work, while others are doing only minimal amounts. For this reason, annual reports should be devoted to brief reports explaining what faculty members have been working on, or, in larger departments, what areas of the department have faculty been working on. Chairs should notify the entire department in writing or in faculty meetings of individual faculty member and student accomplishments. Faculty meetings are particularly good for providing positive reinforcement for typically unrecognized committee work, planning and the like. Such lateral flow helps to build teamwork and morale.

New chairs should develop networks for working with other departments. Often the former chair can provide insight into sources for networking. Networking provides the chair two important sources of information. First, networking provides an *informal* source of information, a way to judge whether the chair's perceptions of events are similar to other chairs' perceptions. Networking provides a way to verify information. Second, networking presents an opportunity to work together with other chairs behind the scenes; decisions and agreements can be made informally and then presented to the appropriate administrator from a position of strength.

Networking often provides departments a chance to work together in novel and supportive ways. For instance, the geology/geography department wishes to begin a program certifying television meterologists. They might consider working with the communication department to lower its costs and produce a better product. Similar kinds of curricula/budget cooperation efforts can be extended among science departments, between science departments and medicine or veterinary medicine or pharmacy. Even relatively unrelated departments such as chemistry and art might find cooperative efforts in a lease-purchase of a copy machine when the two departments are located in the same building. On a practical level, higher level administrators are less willing to axe a proposal from cooperating departments.

UPWARD FLOW

Bureaucracies tend to employ a strict chain of command. In some institutions, a faculty member cannot meet with a dean without either (1) having the chair's permission or (2) discussing a complaint about the chair. It is, therefore, important for a chair to carry legitimate faculty complaints up the line. It is also important for the chair to follow the chain of command. In cases where, for example, the dean states that he or she does not have an additional $4,000 for a faculty position, the chair may ask if the dean would be willing to ask the vice president for the money OR whether the dean would object to the chair's asking the vice president. Instances of going outside the chain of command, even with permission, however, should be rare.

Going outside the established chain of command may pay off once or twice. More often, however, such tactics are seen as undermining the legitimate authority of the superior (a dean, for instance). Most of the time superiors have reasons for permitting chair's to go outside the line of command. Sometimes the reasons can be self-serving; at other times the superior feels the chair can make a better case. However, the new chair should consider two things before attempting to circumvent the superior's authority. First, *how important is it?* Is getting the objective more important now than later objectives, where the dean can help or hinder getting them? Second, is there an *unwritten policy* allowing chairs to go outside the established structure? Is it done often? With what effect? Often information from older or in-place chairs (lateral flow) answers these questions. As a general rule in most bureaucracies, however, it is best to get permission when "circumventing" the chain on command.

An important point to remember is to send positive information up the chain of command. Positive information often serves a public relations function, creating an aura of credibility for the department and the chair. Just as with chairs, as indicated in the Introduction, deans and vice presidents receive few strokes; positive feedback often provides a necessary stroke, one that may be repaid in kind later. The new chair should keep all this in mind when reporting to his or her superiors.

Information Flow in Oral Cultures

A much more difficult process is dealing with information flow in an oral culture. Determining personal from professional facts and separating fact from fiction is often difficult in oral cultures. But as mentioned earlier, most academic institutions are combinations of bureaucracies and oral cultures. For example, at salary raise time, almost every institution in the country becomes an oral culture. Newspapers are ripe with "information," and the rumor mill contains even more diverse sets of data. The types of flow, however, are pretty much the same as they are in a strict bureaucracy: downward flow, lateral flow and upward flow.

DOWNWARD FLOW

Downward flow of information occurs in oral cultures, but often in strange ways. While having an ordinary conversation with a dean, the chair might hear, "I heard Dr. Jones, in your department, is leaving." What kind of response can the chair make? What if this is news to the chair? Does he or she want to appear ignorant? A somewhat innocent question as a response might help the chair gather additional information without divulging any. "What do you mean?" With this question the superior is usually obligated to provide more information, such as where it was heard, who said it, where the person is supposedly going to go, etc. Thus, in dealing with downward communication it is a good idea to ask, *What do you mean?*

The chair, of course, knows what he or she wants to know. For that reason, there are two other questions that need asking, but in a diplomatic manner. The second is, *How do* you know? This question is much too direct for most instances. However, a response such as, "Dr. Jones hasn't said anything to me, yet. Has she said anything to you?" can determine whether the dean's information was gathered firsthand or via some rumor mill.

The third question, and one that must be asked very diplomatically, is *Why are you telling me this?* For example, the dean might be concerned about having to pay travel expenses for incoming candidates to replace Dr. Jones. Or, the dean might wish to offer Jones a counteroffer. Or, it could simply be a means of carrying on the conversation. A diplomatic version might be, "You seem concerned." The dean's response will indicate how important he or she feels about Jones' leaving and may answer the other sorts of questions without delving into the chair's ignorance. However, an honest response seems to work as well, "I haven't heard anything about it." While some administrators may think the chair should know each and every account of each and every faculty member, this is not the norm. Chairs often become paranoid, feeling an obligation to know everything when an honest, "I don't know," often suffices. It is a rare response these days, but one that may gain the chair favor.

Obviously, the problem with downward flow in an oral culture is found in its unpredictability. Superiors often receive informal information that concerns them and they informally let the chair know it. Understand that, as information flows downward, it often loses its factual base. Thus, Dr. Jones indicating that she had been approached by another institution often becomes, "Dr. Jones is leaving for University X." The three questions suggested do much to test the factual base of the information. In some instances, an honest, "I don't know" or "I haven't heard that" is the chair's best and most appropriate response.

LATERAL FLOW

Departmental communication in an oral culture reflects the best and worse of lateral flow. In most departments lateral flow reflects the current social culture. In a sense, the results of lateral flow are greater than the actual messages transmitted. The lateral flow of information within a department is quite difficult for a chair to grasp, especially if the chair stays in the office with his or her door closed. How, then, can the chair discover lateral information?

First, the chair can establish an "open door" policy, at least at certain times of the day. An *open door policy* is one where faculty and students feel they have access to the chair and can discuss problems without interrupting him or her. This is a time when faculty, staff and students can sit down and chat. Information that might normally be suppressed in meetings, for example, often comes up in informal conversations. However, the chair's environment — his or her office — often inhibits communication, especially with the door open. It is, however, a strategy that allows the chair not only to talk with others, but also to catch some of the "gossip" circulating in the halls, from either students or faculty. Sometimes the chair can then "correct" the information before inaccuracies become problem areas.

Second, lateral flow can be discovered by leaving the office and meeting faculty in their environments. Here the chair goes to the faculty member's office or the faculty lounge and "chats" about things. These conversations are not the basis for making decisions, but they allow the chair and faculty members to talk in the confines of their environment, where faculty feel comfortable. Care must be taken not to frequent certain offices more than others, or the slighted will perceive a clique forming. However, as both information gathering and rumor control sessions, such conversations can be beneficial to all.

A third strategy is to engage professional staff in conversation. Since secretaries and other staff members often deal with faculty and students, they are important sources of information. Care must be taken, however, to avoid idle gossiping. Also, much of what the chair tells a staff person in idle conversation becomes grist for the rumor mill later, as the staff person talks with other faculty, staff and students. However, discovering pertinent informal communication helps prevent problems later.

Thus, lateral flow, through an open door policy, talking to faculty in their offices or conversations with staff can be beneficial. Although most of what the chair hears is second or third hand, *how* it is said — and often what is *not* said — provide insight into the department's social culture. Lateral information, found in both oral and bureaucratic cultures, should be an area of focus.

UPWARD FLOW

Upward flow of information is most problematic with information coming from faculty and staff in oral cultures. The chair's job is to keep the dean and others informed on departmental matters, thus upward flow from the chair differs little in bureaucracies or oral cultures. However, conversations with faculty in various contexts provide a variety of information. Some faculty, feeling ill at ease discussing a topic at a meeting, may open up in a one-on-one conversation with the chair. The conversations help the chair realize what kinds of problems the faculty feel are important. Information on "major" problems like assignment of office space, departmental correspondence with alumni, grading practices, standardized testing, etc., often appear to be more important to the faculty than to the chair. Upward flow from faculty helps the chair perceive and act on these problems.

Other Channels (Gossip)

One channel found in any institution is gossip, or grapevine communication. Gossip is usually a lateral form of communication, but it often is viewed as "diagonal." That is, gossip can originate from anywhere in the institution and go anywhere. Although gossip is found predominantly in oral culture (the nature of the information flow in the oral culture supports and encourages gossip), it is found in bureaucracies, too. In bureaucracies the chair must be careful of gossip; typically it is started with some ulterior motive. For instance, gossip about a possible promotion may be someone's way of (1) testing the waters for the promotion or (2) alerting others that so-and-so is thinking about being promoted. Often negative news is "pretested" in gossip networks before being formally announced. In oral cultures, gossip is a way of life and often has as much importance as upward, downward and lateral flow. Chairs need to be careful and find whatever meaning is in the gossip, especially in bureaucracies.

For example, a chair might hear from one of his or her faculty members that a productive junior member of the faculty was preparing to interview at another institution. This information could be accurate or it may merely be a ploy by the faculty member to increase his or her salary. If the information appears correct, the chair could then begin searching for money to counter the expected offers or begin tooling up to search for a replacement. The important thing is that the chair must *verify* the information — gossip about a potential 10% pay raise, when the chair knows the best that can be offered at that time is 5%, is wrong and should be stopped.

Confidential Information

One of the major problems facing a chair is dealing with confidential information. Confidential information is data that may be needed by one person and the chair, but no one else. It is sensitive and could, if made public, embarrass someone. Most confidential information is confidential for a limited time only. Some confidential information remains sensitive for an eternity. Institutions have their own policy on tenure and promotion decisions, for example. Information gathered in making that decision is sensitive and is maintained away from others, to include the person coming up for tenure and promotion. Some institutions, however, open their files to faculty members granted tenure and/or promotion. In this section we attempt to offer some guidelines in those cases where confidentiality policies are less obvious.

Tenure and Promotion

While most academic institutions have a specific policy on the confidentiality of information concerning tenure and

Table B.2
Information Confidentiality

Type of Information	Confidential?
Annual Reports	No
Chair Evaluations of Faculty	Yes
Departmental Budget	No
Faculty Grievance	Yes
Faculty/Staff Salaries	Yes*
Policies	No
Position Advertisements	No
Procedures	No
Student Evaluations of faculty	Yes*
Student Grades	Yes
Student Grievances	Yes

*Some institutions make this information public.

promotion decisions, violations are often observed. In those cases where external letters and/or evaluations are required, those letters should only be made available to the candidate and made available to others on a need-to-know basis and when legally required.* Promotion and tenure committees should stress the confidentiality involved in making decisions *several* times to help prevent violations. Chairs certainly should not discuss tenure and promotion decisions *prior* to the fact; after the decisions have been made, chairs can provide the candidate the decision on a need-to-know timely basis in accordance with institutional policy. General office discussions about tenure and promotion decisions should not occur. This confidentiality is for the protection of both candidate and chair (in the event of a grievance proceeding or law suit).

Students' Grades

Students' grades are confidential and access is based only on a need-to-know basis. Some faculty believe it is appropriate to discuss "good grades," however, students' grades are *their* properties. Therefore, faculty should not hand papers to students' roommates, or discuss a grade with a parent or potential employer over the telephone, etc. When records are kept in a departmental office, they are available to the student's advisor only. Some faculty feel they have a right to check a student's overall records against that student's grade in his or her class. This simply is not true. Posting of grades should be kept to a minimum and in accordance with the law. Students have no right to know what grade another student made in a class, even during a student grade grievance.

Student Complaints

Some institutions have specific guidelines for handling student complaints about faculty members. In such cases, the chair should be familiar with both the institution's student and faculty handbooks. These handbooks provide guidelines and definitions for student complaints. Other institutions offer no specific procedure for handling student complaints about a faculty member. The following is a suggested procedure. In either case, it is preferable that the chair attempt to arbitrate the problem before allowing it to go to a higher level.

If the chair feels a student's complaint is a case where a slight delay might solve the problem, a cooling off period should be proposed. Having the student to set up an appointment a day or two later will lessen the emotional furor and may even cause the student to change his or her mind. When the student comes back to the chair's office, it should be ascertained if he or she has discussed the complaint with the faculty in question. If the answer is, "no," then the chair should suggest that the student and faculty member might work out the problem together. However, as is often the case, if the student is afraid of a one-on-one confrontation with the faculty, the chair should explain that there will have to be a meeting among the chair, the student and the faculty member.

This meeting is a formal fact-finding discussion where the chair attempts to have all of the information aired with opinions separated from facts. At the earliest possible date after the meeting, the chair notifies the student and the faculty member of his or her decision. In those rare cases when the student is still dissatisfied with the decision, the chair will notify the student of his or her rights in accordance with any established grievance procedure. The complaint itself, the decision, the results, etc., are confidential information and must be kept between the parties involved. There is no reason or point in providing this information to other faculty or students. Both the student and faculty member must be made aware of the confidentiality of the meeting and the decision.

Faculty Complaints

When a faculty member complains about a chair, a similar procedure is employed. In this case the chair takes great care to gather as much information as possible. Again, the information is kept confidential by both chair and faculty member. If the faculty member feels intimidated by the chair, the dean is asked to serve as arbitrator. If the faculty member is dissatisfied with the decision, he or she should be informed of whatever grievance procedure the institution has and his or her rights under that procedure.

Faculty Evaluations, Annual Reviews, Salaries

Obviously, the chair should consider faculty evaluations, annual reviews and salary reviews confidential, unless institutional policy states otherwise. Some universities and colleges publish salaries; some allow anyone to read faculty evaluations and reviews; institutional policy governs when information is *NOT* confidential. However, the chair should always remember when evaluating a faculty member that the individual is being evaluated as a single entity. Therefore, what the chair writes on someone else's evaluation is as confidential as what he or she writes on the other's evaluation (at least up to that point where the institution says it is otherwise).

Principles of Effective Communication Management

From the previous chapters and appendices fifteen principles of communication management can be deduced. By keeping these principles in mind, the academic department chair is better able to communicate with — to lead — his or her various constituencies.

1. The chair should be organized in his or her access to information. Data should be accurate, complete and up-to-date.

2. The chair should be redundant in providing information to others, especially when the information is negative.

3. The chair should recognize that he or she wears different hats and must play many roles, sometimes extremely diverse roles within minutes of one another.

4. To have *effective* relationships with the faculty and staff, chairs should be fair, honest and open with faculty. The personality of the individual will determine how personally close the chair is to the faculty and staff, but fairness will determine the degree of respect that he or she receives.

5. Confidentiality and integrity are important attributes of the chair. The chair must learn what information is to be kept close to the vest.

6. In communicating with administrative peers, the chair should learn that in the long run cooperation wins out against competition every time. Especially when the economics of higher education are less than what are needed, cooperation is essential.

7. In managing grievances the chair must be both objective and empathic. He or she must understand that the reasons behind complaints are varied and often understanding is more important than resolution.

8. The budget process only works when information is shared and decisions are objective.

9. In assessing faculty, the chair should remember that assessment is an ongoing, daily activity. Faculty and staff like to be assessed, they like to know where they stand and they like to know what they need to do to improve.

10. When chairs are being assessed they need to learn not to be defensive. An assessment is a learning process.

11. When the department is being assessed, the chair needs to inform all concerned as completely as possible. Most assessments ultimately benefit the department.

12. Motivating faculty is primarily a skill of understanding not only what a chair wants from the faculty but what the faculty wants from the chair.

13. A department that is open may well be a department that is productive. The word spreads when a department is doing well. The rich get richer.

14. A department's ethos is based on a number of factors which show the world that the department: (1) cares about its students, (2) works hard, (3) gets along with others inside the department and (4) cooperates with others outside the department.

15. Optimism, trust and sense of humor bring about many more resources than do their opposites.

---

*For an example, see: University of Pennsylvania vs. Equal Employment Opportunity Commission (1990).

Contributors

Ronald L. Applbaum (Ph.D., Pennsylvania State University) is president of Westfield State College. He was previously Vice President for Academic Affairs at the University of Texas — Pan American, and Dean of Humanities and Associate Dean of Letters at California State University, Long Beach. Applbaum has coauthored eight books and authored numerous articles on topics ranging from organizational communication to communication education to research methodology. He is Secretary General of the World Communication Association.

Carla Bennett (M.A., Midwestern State University) is assistant professor of Mass Communication at Midwestern State University. She has received an *Addy Award* for excellence in advertising. In addition, she has produced a number of television programs and public relations television campaigns for her university and community.

Stanley A. Deetz (Ph.D., Ohio University) is professor in the Department of Communication, Rutgers University. Deetz was the chair of the department at Rutgers from 1985 through 1988. His research has focused on the significance of ethics, power and conflict in the organizational context. His publications have appeared in the

225

disciplines of management and sociology, as well as communication. He has also served as editor of *Communication Yearbook*

Patti Peete Gillespie (Ph.D., Indiana University) is professor and chair, Department of Communication Arts and Theatre, University of Maryland. She has a number of publications in the performing arts, including three coauthored books. She is former president of the Association of Communication Administration (ACA), the Speech Communication Association (SCA), and is a consultant for both.

Mark Hickson III (Ph.D., Southern Illinois University) is professor and chair of the Department of Communication Studies at the University of Alabama at Birmingham. Previously he was chair at Mississippi State University. Hickson was the founding editor of the *Journal of Applied Communication Research* and has coauthored three books on communication. He is a consultant for the Association for Communication Administration and the Speech Communication Association. He is co-editor of *World Communication.*

Fred E. Jandt (Ph.D., Bowling Green State University) is professor and founding chair, Department of Communication, California State University at San Bernardino. Formerly, he was Director of Faculty Development at Sate University of New York College at Brockport. He is the author of *Conflict Resolution Through Communication* and *Win-Win Negotiating: Turning Conflict Into Agreement.*

June Kable (Ed.D., North Texas State University) is Director of the Division of Fine Arts at Midwestern State University. She is coauthor (with Victoria O'Donnell) of *Persuasion: An Interactive-Dependence Approach.* She has been a reviewer for Random House and Wadsworth Publishing Company. She is past president of the Texas Speech Communication Association.

John A. Kaufman (Ph.D., Michigan State University) is associate professor Department of Communication, California State Polytechnic University, Pomona. He has been a contributor to *Public Relations Review, Newspaper Research Journal* and other communication journals.

Susan K. Kovar (Ph.D., University of Minnesota) is associate professor of Physical Education and chair of the Division of Health, Physical Education, and Recreation at Emporia State University. She has published a number of articles about physical education, administration, and faculty development.

James C. McCroskey (Ed.D., Pennsylvania State University) is professor and chair of the Department of Communication Studies at West Virginia University. He has published over twenty books and more than one hundred articles in various journals. He has served as vice president of the International Communication and the World Communication Association and as president of the Eastern Communication Association. He has been editor of *Communication Education, Human Communication Research*, and has served on the editorial boards of fifteen other journals.

Edward L. McGlone (Ph.D., Ohio University) is professor of Communication and Director of Research for the School of Library and Information Management at Emporia State University. He has served previously as a department chair, and arts and sciences dean, and an academic vice president. He has published articles in the *Modern Language Journal, Communication Education,* and the *Association for Communication Administration Bulletin*, to name a few.

Virginia P. Richmond (Ph.D., University of Nebraska) is professor and director of Graduate Programs in Communication Studies at West Virginia University. She has been published in *Human Communication Research, Communication Education, Communication*

Quarterly, and other journals in communication, pharmacy and chiropractics. She is former editor of *Communication Research Reports* and is the current editor of *Communication Quarterly.*

Randall K. Scott (Ph.D., University of Southern Mississippi) is assistant professor of Communication Studies at the University of Alabama at Birmingham. He has been published in *Journalism Quarterly* and *Psychological Reports.* He is director of the broadcasting area at the University of Alabama at Birmingham.

Robert M. Smith (Ph.D., Temple University) is Dean of the School of Arts and Sciences at the University of Tennessee at Martin. Previously he served in various administrative capacities at Wichita State University. He has been published in numerous journals in the communication discipline. He is former president of the Association for Communication Administration.

Christopher H. Spicer (Ph.D., University of Texas) is professor and chair of the Communication Arts Department at Pacific Lutheran University. He teaches and consults in public relations and organizational communication. He has been published in *Educational Administration Quarterly, Communication Education, ACA Bulletin* and *Clues: A Journal of Detection.*

Don W. Stacks (Ph.D., University of Florida) is associate professor of Communication at the University of Miami. He has published in interpersonal communication, intrapersonal communication, communication education, public relations, advertising and organizational communication. He has co-authored four books. He serves as a program consultant for the Speech Communication Association and is a certified arbitrator.

Michael Stano (Ph.D., University of Minnesota; J.D., Oklahoma City University) is associate professor of Speech Communication at Oklahoma State University. He has written numerous publications in interviewing and performance appraisal. His consulting in this area has spanned such firms as Shell Oil Company, Xerox Corporation, the United States Army, Blue Cross-Blue Shield, the American Association of Medical Assistants and Honeywell.

Ann Q. Staton (Ph.D., University of Texas) is professor and chair of the Department of Speech Communication, University of Washington. Her interest is in instructional communication and her work appears in journals such as *Communication Education, Human Communication Research,* and *Educational Administration Quarterly.* She just completed *Communication and Student Socialization,* a book about socialization throughout the student's career.

Anita Taylor (Ph.D., University of Missouri) is professor of Communication at George Mason University where she chaired the Communication Department and the Department of Fine and Performing Arts and Communication. She previously was Associate Dean of the Arts and Communications Division at the St. Louis Community College at Florissant Valley and also has chaired its department of Speech and Theatre. She has served as president of both the Association for Communication Administration and the Speech Communication Association and is now editor of the research periodical, *Women and Language.*

Index

Academic freedom, 68
Administration, 42; deans, 83–85, decision-making, 45–50; departmental, 146–147; structure, 45–50
Advising, 198–199
American Association of University Professors (AAUP), 60–61
American Council on Education (ACE), 80
Authority, 171–172

Behavioral alteration techniques (BATs), 163–165
Budget, 81–88, 196–197; and faculty, 85–88
Bureaucratic model, 208–214

Collective bargaining, 62
Collegial model, 2, 28, 53
Complaints: faculty, 66–70, 221; resolution, 75–76; student, 30–33, 62–66, 220–221
Compliance gaining, 160
Confidentiality, 218–221
Culture, 1–4; oral, 214–217
Curricula, 148–150

Evaluation, 55; chairs, 121–140; departments, 143–158; faculty, 92–105; fairness, 108–110;

instruments, 128–137; interviews, 107–118; scheduling, 111; student, 150–151
Experts, 154–155

Faculty: adjunct, 35–36; motivating, 159–182; relationships with staff, 36–37

Grievance procedures, 70–74

Harassment, 32, 66
Hiring, 161–162

Industrial model, 2
Integrity, 30

Leadership, 6, 14, 24–25, 54, 124–127

Mission: institutional, 82

Power: invisible, 8–10; position, 27
Promotion, 69–70
Public relations, 183–194
Punishment, 167–170

Rewards, 11–12, 55, 165–167, 180–181

Salary, 177
Staff, 25, 37–38

Tenure, 69–70, 218–219